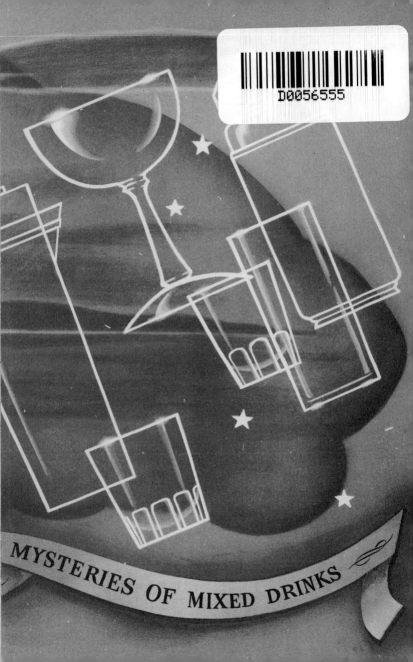

MYSTERIES OF MIXED DRINKS

OLD MR. BOSTO

De Luxe

OFFICIAL
BARTENDER'S
GUIDE

Compiled and Edited by Leo Cotton
in collaboration with Old Time Boston Bartenders
for
BEN BURK INC., BOSTON

Libby dear:-

Louis said
to tell you not to try
drinking all these
concoctions at the same
time.

Laura Pelton
3/21/45

Foreword

I N 1935, the first edition of the OLD MR. BOSTON
DELUXE OFFICIAL BARTENDER'S GUIDE
was published to provide a cocktail and recipe book
that would be authentic and accurate.

It was dedicated to the thousands of bartenders
throughout the country and to that part of the American
public which desired a truly official source of informa-
tion for home mixing.

The gratifying enthusiasm with which the completely
revised 4th edition was received has necessitated the
printing of this new edition.

The 5th edition has been further expanded with the
addition of a new, colorful sixteen-page insert, beauti-
fully illustrating the most popular mixed drinks, together
with suggestions for some very appetizing and simple to
make hors d'ouevres.

The Editor, once again, wishes to acknowledge his
appreciation to Joseph DeSoto, founder and chief in-
structor of the original Boston Bartenders' School; Chris
Lane, secretary of the Boston Bartenders' Union; Joseph
Miron, John R. Fitzpatrick and Thomas J. Kane; all
bartenders of the old school and authorities in the art
of mixing drinks.

L. C.

Sirs:—May we now present to you Old Mr. Boston in permanent form. We know you are going to like him. He is a jolly fellow, one of those rare individuals, everlastingly young, a distinct personality and famous throughout the land for his sterling qualities and genuine good fellowship. His friends number in the millions those who are great and those who are near great even as you and I. He is joyful and ever ready to accept the difficult role of "Life of the Party", a sympathetic friend who may be relied upon in any emergency . . . Follow his advice and there will be many pleasant times in store for you.

Gentlemen, Old Mr. Boston.

INDEX

5

INDEX

COCKTAILS
WITH BRANDY
(Blackberry)

COCKTAILS
WITH BRANDY
(Peach)

COCKTAILS
WITH BRANDY
(Wild Cherry)

COCKTAILS
WITH CHAMPAGNE

COCKTAILS
WITH CREME DE CACAO

COCKTAILS
WITH
CREME DE MENTHE

7

INDEX

INDEX

INDEX

COCKTAILS
WITH DUBONNET

COCKTAILS
WITH KUMMEL

COCKTAILS
WITH NECTAR LIQUEUR

COCKTAILS
WITH
ORANGE FLAVORED GIN

INDEX

INDEX

13

14

INDEX

A

ABBEY COCKTAIL

1 1/2 oz. Old Mr. Boston Dry Gin
    Juice of 1/4 Orange
1 Dash Orange Bitters
Shake well with cracked Ice and strain into 3 oz. Cocktail glass. Add a Maraschino Cherry.

ABSINTHE
COCKTAIL

1 1/2 oz. Absinthe Substitute
3/4 oz. Water
1/4 oz. Old Mr. Boston Anisette
1 Dash Orange Bitters
Shake well with cracked Ice and strain into 3 oz. Cocktail glass.

ABSINTHE DRIP
COCKTAIL

1 1/2 oz. Absinthe Substitute
Dissolve 1 lump of Sugar, using the French drip spoon, and fill glass with cold water. Use Old Fashioned Cocktail glass.

ABSINTHE
SPECIAL
COCKTAIL

1 1/2 oz. Absinthe Substitute
1 oz. Water
1/4 Teaspoon Powdered Sugar
1 Dash Orange Bitters
Shake well with cracked Ice and strain into 3 oz. Cocktall glass.

ADONIS COCKTAIL

1 Dash Orange Bitters
3/4 oz. Italian Vermouth
1 1/2 oz. Dry Sherry
Stir well with cracked Ice and strain into 3 oz. Cocktail glass.

AFFINITY
COCKTAIL

3/4 oz. French Vermouth
3/4 oz. Italian Vermouth
3/4 oz. Scotch Whiskey
2 Dashes Orange Bitters
Stir well with cracked Ice and strain into 3 oz. Cocktail glass.

A

1 oz. Old Mr. Boston Apricot Flavored Brandy
1 oz. Old Mr. Boston Curacao
1/2 Teaspoon Lemon Juice
Shake well with cracked Ice and strain into 3 oz. Cocktail glass.

AFTER DINNER
COCKTAIL

1 oz. Old Mr. Boston Apricot Flavored Brandy
1 oz. Old Mr. Boston Curacao
1/2 Teaspoon Lemon Juice
Shake well with cracked Ice and strain into 3 oz. Cocktail glass.

AFTER SUPPER
COCKTAIL

1/2 oz. Lemon Juice
1/2 Teaspoon Powdered Sugar
1 1/2 oz. Old Mr. Boston California Brandy
1 Teaspoon Old Mr. Boston Curacao
Shake well with cracked Ice and strain into 3 oz. Cocktail glass.

ALABAMA
COCKTAIL

Juice 1/2 Lemon
1 Teaspoon Powdered Sugar
2 oz. Old Mr. Boston Dry Gin
Shake well with cracked Ice and strain into 7 oz. Highball glass. Fill with Carbonated Water. Add 2 Sprigs of Fresh Mint.

ALABAMA FIZZ

2 Dashes Orange Bitters
1 1/2 oz. Old Mr. Boston Dry Gin
3/4 oz. Yellow Chartreuse
Stir well with cracked Ice and strain into 3 oz. Cocktail glass.

ALASKA COCKTAIL

Juice 1/2 Lemon
1 Teaspoon Powdered Sugar
2 oz. Old Mr. Boston Dry Gin
Shake well with cracked Ice and strain into 7 oz. Highball glass. Fill with Carbonated Water. Add 1 Teaspoon Raspberry Syrup.

ALBEMARLE FIZZ

17

A

ALEXANDER
COCKTAIL No. 1

1 oz. Old Mr. Boston Dry Gin
1 oz. Old Mr. Boston Creme de Cacao
1 oz. Sweet Cream
Shake well with cracked Ice and strain
into 4 oz. Cocktail glass.

ALEXANDER
COCKTAIL No. 2

1 oz. Old Mr. Boston Creme de Cacao
1 oz. Old Mr. Boston California
 Brandy
1 oz. Sweet Cream
Shake well with cracked Ice and strain
into 4 oz. Cocktail glass.

ALEXANDER'S
SISTER COCKTAIL

1 oz. Old Mr. Boston Dry Gin
1 oz. Old Mr. Boston Creme de
 Menthe
1 oz. Sweet Cream
Shake well with cracked Ice and strain
into 4 oz. Cocktail glass.

ALLEN COCKTAIL

1/4 Teaspoon Lemon Juice
3/4 oz. Maraschino
1 1/2 oz. Old Mr. Boston Dry Gin
Shake well with cracked Ice and strain
into 3 oz. Cocktail glass.

ALLIES COCKTAIL

1 oz. French Vermouth
1 oz. Old Mr. Boston Dry Gin
1/2 Teaspoon Old Mr. Boston Kummel
Shake well with cracked Ice and strain
into 3 oz. Cocktail glass.

AMER PICON
COCKTAIL

Juice 1 Lime
1 Teaspoon Grenadine
1 1/2 oz. Amer Picon
Shake well with cracked Ice and strain
into 3 oz. Cocktail glass.

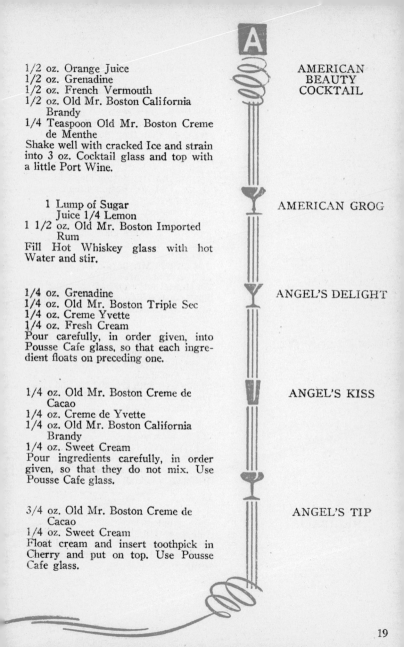

1/2 oz. Orange Juice
1/2 oz. Grenadine
1/2 oz. French Vermouth
1/2 oz. Old Mr. Boston California
        Brandy
1/4 Teaspoon Old Mr. Boston Creme
        de Menthe
Shake well with cracked Ice and strain
into 3 oz. Cocktail glass and top with
a little Port Wine.

AMERICAN BEAUTY COCKTAIL

1 Lump of Sugar
  Juice 1/4 Lemon
1 1/2 oz. Old Mr. Boston Imported
        Rum
Fill Hot Whiskey glass with hot
Water and stir.

AMERICAN GROG

1/4 oz. Grenadine
1/4 oz. Old Mr. Boston Triple Sec
1/4 oz. Creme Yvette
1/4 oz. Fresh Cream
Pour carefully, in order given, into
Pousse Cafe glass, so that each ingredient floats on preceding one.

ANGEL'S DELIGHT

1/4 oz. Old Mr. Boston Creme de
        Cacao
1/4 oz. Creme de Yvette
1/4 oz. Old Mr. Boston California
        Brandy
1/4 oz. Sweet Cream
Pour ingredients carefully, in order
given, so that they do not mix. Use
Pousse Cafe glass.

ANGEL'S KISS

3/4 oz. Old Mr. Boston Creme de
        Cacao
1/4 oz. Sweet Cream
Float cream and insert toothpick in
Cherry and put on top. Use Pousse
Cafe glass.

ANGEL'S TIP

19

A

ANGEL'S WING

1/3 oz. Old Mr. Boston Creme de Cacao
1/3 oz. Old Mr. Boston California Brandy
1/3 oz. Sweet Cream
Pour ingredients carefully, in order given, so that they do not mix. Use Pousse Cafe glass.

APPARENT COCKTAIL

1 oz. Old Mr. Boston Dry Gin
1 oz. Old Mr. Boston Creme de Cacao
1/4 Teaspoon Absinthe substitute
Shake well with cracked Ice and strain into 3 oz. Cocktail glass.

APPETIZER COCKTAIL

3/4 oz. Old Mr. Boston Dry Gin
3/4 oz. Dubonnet
Juice of 1/4 Orange
Shake well with cracked Ice and strain into 3 oz. Cocktail glass.

APPLE BLOW FIZZ

White of 1 Egg
Juice 1/2 Lemon
1 Teaspoon Powdered Sugar
2 oz. Applejack
Shake well with cracked Ice and strain into 8 oz. Highball glass. Fill with Carbonated Water.

APPLEJACK COCKTAIL

1 1/2 oz. Applejack
1 Teaspoon Grenadine
1 Teaspoon Lemon Juice
Shake well with cracked Ice and strain into 3 oz. Cocktail glass.

APPLEJACK HIGHBALL

1 Cube of Ice
2 oz. Applejack
Fill 8 oz. Highball glass with Ginger Ale or Carbonated Water. Add Twist of Lemon Peel, if desired, and stir gently.

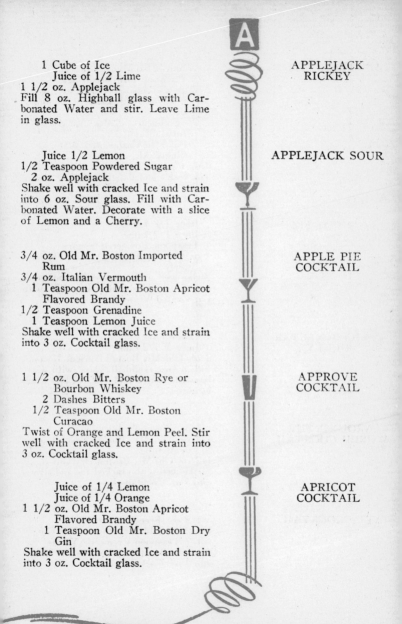

A

APPLEJACK
RICKEY

1 Cube of Ice
Juice of 1/2 Lime
1 1/2 oz. Applejack
Fill 8 oz. Highball glass with Carbonated Water and stir. Leave Lime in glass.

APPLEJACK SOUR

Juice 1/2 Lemon
1/2 Teaspoon Powdered Sugar
2 oz. Applejack
Shake well with cracked Ice and strain into 6 oz. Sour glass. Fill with Carbonated Water. Decorate with a slice of Lemon and a Cherry.

APPLE PIE
COCKTAIL

3/4 oz. Old Mr. Boston Imported
Rum
3/4 oz. Italian Vermouth
1 Teaspoon Old Mr. Boston Apricot
Flavored Brandy
1/2 Teaspoon Grenadine
1 Teaspoon Lemon Juice
Shake well with cracked Ice and strain into 3 oz. Cocktail glass.

APPROVE
COCKTAIL

1 1/2 oz. Old Mr. Boston Rye or
Bourbon Whiskey
2 Dashes Bitters
1/2 Teaspoon Old Mr. Boston
Curacao
Twist of Orange and Lemon Peel. Stir well with cracked Ice and strain into 3 oz. Cocktail glass.

APRICOT
COCKTAIL

Juice of 1/4 Lemon
Juice of 1/4 Orange
1 1/2 oz. Old Mr. Boston Apricot
Flavored Brandy
1 Teaspoon Old Mr. Boston Dry
Gin
Shake well with cracked Ice and strain into 3 oz. Cocktail glass.

A

APRICOT COOLER

Into 12 oz. Tom Collins glass, put:
1/2 Teaspoon Powdered Sugar
2 oz. Carbonated Water, and stir.
Fill glass with Cracked Ice and add:
2 oz. Old Mr. Boston Apricot Flavored Brandy.
Fill with Carbonated Water or Ginger Ale.
Insert spiral of Orange or Lemon Peel (or both) and dangle end over rim of glass.

APRICOT FIZZ

Juice 1/2 Lemon
Juice 1/2 Lime
1 Teaspoon Powdered Sugar
2 oz. Old Mr. Boston Apricot Flavored Brandy
Shake well with cracked Ice and strain into 7 oz. Highball glass. Fill with Carbonated Water.

APRICOT NECTAR RICKEY

1 Cube of Ice
Juice of 1/2 Lime
2 oz. Old Mr. Boston Apricot Nectar
Fill 8 oz. Highball glass with Carbonated Water and stir. Leave Lime in glass.

AROUND THE WORLD COCKTAIL

1 oz. Pineapple Juice
1/2 oz. Old Mr. Boston Green Creme de Menthe
1/2 oz. Old Mr. Boston Dry Gin
Shake well with cracked Ice and strain into 3 oz. Cocktail glass.

ATTY COCKTAIL

1/2 oz. French Vermouth
1 1/2 oz. Old Mr. Boston Dry Gin
1/2 Teaspoon Creme de Yvette
Shake well with cracked Ice and strain into 3 oz. Cocktail glass.

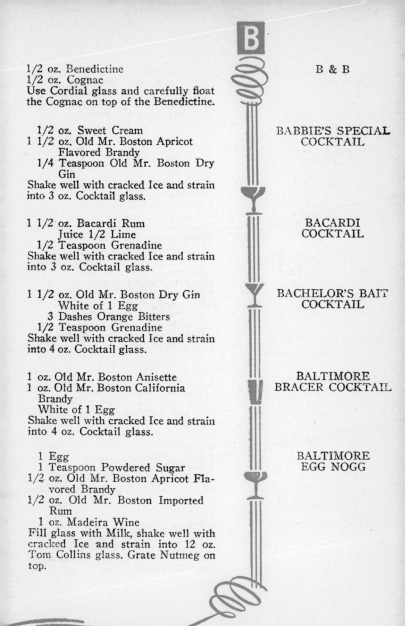

B

1/2 oz. Benedictine
1/2 oz. Cognac
Use Cordial glass and carefully float
the Cognac on top of the Benedictine.

B & B

1/2 oz. Sweet Cream
1 1/2 oz. Old Mr. Boston Apricot
    Flavored Brandy
1/4 Teaspoon Old Mr. Boston Dry
    Gin
Shake well with cracked Ice and strain
into 3 oz. Cocktail glass.

BABBIE'S SPECIAL
COCKTAIL

1 1/2 oz. Bacardi Rum
    Juice 1/2 Lime
1/2 Teaspoon Grenadine
Shake well with cracked Ice and strain
into 3 oz. Cocktail glass.

BACARDI
COCKTAIL

1 1/2 oz. Old Mr. Boston Dry Gin
    White of 1 Egg
    3 Dashes Orange Bitters
1/2 Teaspoon Grenadine
Shake well with cracked Ice and strain
into 4 oz. Cocktail glass.

BACHELOR'S BAIT
COCKTAIL

1 oz. Old Mr. Boston Anisette
1 oz. Old Mr. Boston California
    Brandy
    White of 1 Egg
Shake well with cracked Ice and strain
into 4 oz. Cocktail glass.

BALTIMORE
BRACER COCKTAIL

1 Egg
1 Teaspoon Powdered Sugar
1/2 oz. Old Mr. Boston Apricot Fla-
    vored Brandy
1/2 oz. Old Mr. Boston Imported
    Rum
1 oz. Madeira Wine
Fill glass with Milk, shake well with
cracked Ice and strain into 12 oz.
Tom Collins glass. Grate Nutmeg on
top.

BALTIMORE
EGG NOGG

B

BAMBOO
COCKTAIL

1 1/2 oz. Sherry
3/4 oz. French Vermouth
1 Dash Orange Bitters
Stir well with cracked Ice and strain
into 3 oz. Cocktail glass.

BARBARY COAST
COCKTAIL

1/2 oz. Old Mr. Boston Dry Gin
1/2 oz. Old Mr. Boston Imported
Rum
1/2 oz. Old Mr. Boston Creme de
Cacao
1/2 oz. Scotch Whiskey
1/2 oz. Sweet Cream
Shake well with cracked Ice and strain
into 4 oz. Cocktail glass.

BARON COCKTAIL

1/2 oz. French Vermouth
1 1/2 oz. Old Mr. Boston Dry Gin
1 1/2 Teaspoons Old Mr. Boston
Curacao
1/2 Teaspoon Italian Vermouth
Stir well with cracked Ice and strain
into 3 oz. Cocktail glass. Add twist of
Lemon Peel and drop in glass.

BARTON SPECIAL
COCKTAIL

1/2 oz. Apple Brandy
1/2 oz. Scotch Whiskey
1 1/2 oz. Old Mr. Boston Dry Gin
Stir well with cracked Ice and strain
into 3 oz. Cocktail glass.

BEADLESTONE
COCKTAIL

1 1/4 oz. French Vermouth
1 1/4 oz. Scotch Whiskey
Stir well with cracked Ice and strain
into 3 oz. Cocktail glass.

BEALS COCKTAIL

1 1/2 oz. Scotch Whiskey
1/2 oz. French Vermouth
1/2 oz. Italian Vermouth
Stir well with cracked Ice and strain
into 3 oz. Cocktail glass.

24

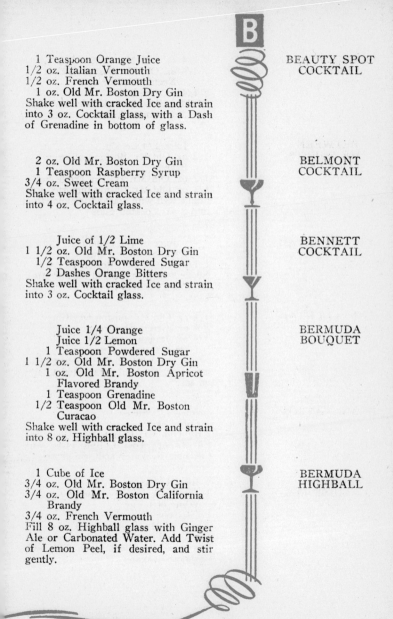

1 Teaspoon Orange Juice
1/2 oz. Italian Vermouth
1/2 oz. French Vermouth
1 oz. Old Mr. Boston Dry Gin
Shake well with cracked Ice and strain
into 3 oz. Cocktail glass, with a Dash
of Grenadine in bottom of glass.

BEAUTY SPOT COCKTAIL

2 oz. Old Mr. Boston Dry Gin
1 Teaspoon Raspberry Syrup
3/4 oz. Sweet Cream
Shake well with cracked Ice and strain
into 4 oz. Cocktail glass.

BELMONT COCKTAIL

Juice of 1/2 Lime
1 1/2 oz. Old Mr. Boston Dry Gin
1/2 Teaspoon Powdered Sugar
2 Dashes Orange Bitters
Shake well with cracked Ice and strain
into 3 oz. Cocktail glass.

BENNETT COCKTAIL

Juice 1/4 Orange
Juice 1/2 Lemon
1 Teaspoon Powdered Sugar
1 1/2 oz. Old Mr. Boston Dry Gin
1 oz. Old Mr. Boston Apricot
    Flavored Brandy
1 Teaspoon Grenadine
1/2 Teaspoon Old Mr. Boston
    Curacao
Shake well with cracked Ice and strain
into 8 oz. Highball glass.

BERMUDA BOUQUET

1 Cube of Ice
3/4 oz. Old Mr. Boston Dry Gin
3/4 oz. Old Mr. Boston California
    Brandy
3/4 oz. French Vermouth
Fill 8 oz. Highball glass with Ginger
Ale or Carbonated Water. Add Twist
of Lemon Peel, if desired, and stir
gently.

BERMUDA HIGHBALL

25

B

BERMUDA ROSE COCKTAIL

1 1/4 oz. Old Mr. Boston Dry Gin
1/4 oz. Old Mr. Boston Apricot Nectar Liqueur
1/4 oz. Grenadine
Shake well with cracked Ice and strain into 3 oz. Cocktail glass.

BETWEEN THE SHEETS COCKTAIL

Juice 1/4 Lemon
1/2 oz. Old Mr. Boston California Brandy
1/2 oz. Old Mr. Boston Triple Sec
1/2 oz. Old Mr. Boston Imported Rum
Shake well with cracked Ice and strain into 3 oz. Cocktail glass.

BIFFY COCKTAIL

Juice of 1/2 Lemon
1/2 oz. Swedish Punch
1 1/2 oz. Old Mr. Boston Dry Gin
Shake well with cracked Ice and strain into 3 oz. Cocktail glass.

BIJOU COCKTAIL

3/4 oz. Old Mr. Boston Dry Gin
3/4 oz. Green Chartreuse
3/4 oz. Italian Vermouth
1 Dash Orange Bitters
Shake well with cracked Ice and strain into 3 oz. Cocktail glass. Add Cherry on top.

BILLY TAYLOR

Juice 1/2 Lime
2 Cubes of Ice
2 oz. Old Mr. Boston Dry Gin
Fill 12 oz. Tom Collins glass with Carbonated Water and stir gently.

BIRD OF PARADISE FIZZ

Juice 1/2 Lemon
1 Teaspoon Powdered Sugar
White of 1 Egg
1 Teaspoon Grenadine
2 oz. Old Mr. Boston Dry Gin
Shake well with cracked Ice and strain into 8 oz. Highball glass. Fill with Carbonated Water.

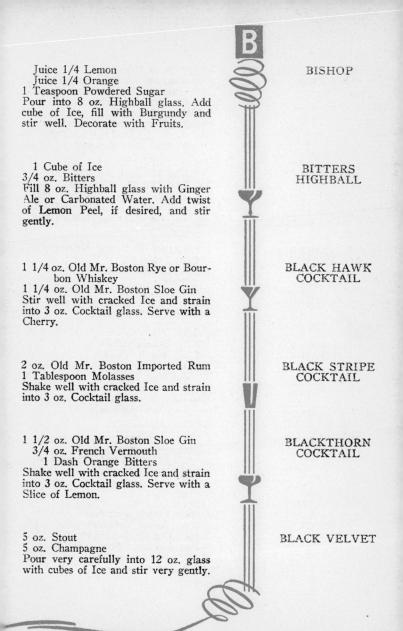

B

Juice 1/4 Lemon
Juice 1/4 Orange
1 Teaspoon Powdered Sugar
Pour into 8 oz. Highball glass. Add cube of Ice, fill with Burgundy and stir well. Decorate with Fruits.

BISHOP

1 Cube of Ice
3/4 oz. Bitters
Fill 8 oz. Highball glass with Ginger Ale or Carbonated Water. Add twist of **Lemon** Peel, if desired, and stir gently.

BITTERS
HIGHBALL

1 1/4 oz. Old Mr. Boston Rye or Bourbon Whiskey
1 1/4 oz. Old Mr. Boston Sloe Gin
Stir well with cracked Ice and strain into 3 oz. Cocktail glass. Serve with a Cherry.

BLACK HAWK
COCKTAIL

2 oz. Old Mr. Boston Imported Rum
1 Tablespoon Molasses
Shake well with cracked Ice and strain into 3 oz. Cocktail glass.

BLACK STRIPE
COCKTAIL

1 1/2 oz. Old Mr. Boston Sloe Gin
3/4 oz. French Vermouth
1 Dash Orange Bitters
Shake well with cracked Ice and strain into 3 oz. Cocktail glass. Serve with a Slice of Lemon.

BLACKTHORN
COCKTAIL

5 oz. Stout
5 oz. Champagne
Pour very carefully into 12 oz. glass with cubes of Ice and stir very gently.

BLACK VELVET

B

BLARNEY STONE COCKTAIL

2 oz. Irish Whiskey
1/2 Teaspoon Absinthe Substitute
1/2 Teaspoon Old Mr. Boston Curacao
1/4 Teaspoon Maraschino
1 Dash Bitters
Shake well with cracked Ice and strain into 3 oz. Cocktail glass. Twist of Orange Peel and serve with an Olive.

BLENTON COCKTAIL

3/4 oz. French Vermouth
1 1/2 oz. Old Mr. Boston Dry Gin
1 Dash Orange Bitters.
Stir well with cracked Ice and strain into 3 oz. Cocktail glass. Add a Cherry.

BLOCK AND FALL COCKTAIL

1/4 oz. Old Mr. Boston Anisette
1/4 oz. Applejack
3/4 oz. Old Mr. Boston California Brandy
3/4 oz. Old Mr. Boston Triple Sec
Shake well with cracked Ice and strain into 3 oz. Cocktail glass.

BLOOD AND SAND COCKTAIL

1/2 oz. Orange Juice
1/2 oz. Scotch Whiskey
1/2 oz. Old Mr. Boston Wild Cherry Flavored Brandy
1/2 oz. Italian Vermouth
Shake well with cracked Ice and strain into 3 oz. Cocktail glass.

BLOOD BRONX COCKTAIL

1 1/2 oz. Old Mr. Boston Dry Gin
1/4 oz. French Vermouth
Juice of 1/4 Blood Orange
Shake well with cracked Ice and strain into 3 oz. Cocktail glass.

BLOODHOUND COCKTAIL

1/2 oz. French Vermouth
1/2 oz. Italian Vermouth
1 oz. Old Mr. Boston Dry Gin
2 or 3 crushed Strawberries
Shake well with cracked Ice and strain into 3 oz. Cocktail glass.

BLUE BLAZER

Use two large silver-plated mugs, with handles.
2 1/2 oz. Old Mr. Boston Rye or
        Bourbon Whiskey
2 1/2 oz. Boiling Water
Put the whiskey into one mug, and the boiling water into the other, ignite the whiskey and, while blazing, mix both ingredients by pouring them four or five times from one mug to the other. If well done, this will have the appearance of a continued stream of liquid fire.
Sweeten with 1 teaspoon of Powdered Sugar and serve with a piece of Lemon Peel. Serve in 4 oz. Hot Whiskey glass.

BLUE DEVIL COCKTAIL

1 oz. Old Mr. Boston Dry Gin
    Juice 1/2 Lemon or 1 Lime
1/2 oz. Maraschino
1/2 Teaspoon Creme de Yvette
Shake well with cracked Ice and strain into 3 oz. Cocktail glass.

BLUE MOON COCKTAIL

1 1/2 oz. Old Mr. Boston Dry Gin
    3/4 oz. Creme de Yvette
Shake well with cracked Ice and strain into 3 oz. Cocktail glass. Add twist of Lemon Peel and drop in glass.

BOBBY BURNS COCKTAIL

1 1/4 oz. Italian Vermouth
1 1/4 oz. Scotch Whiskey
    1 Teaspoon Benedictine
Stir well with cracked Ice and strain into 3 oz. Cocktail glass. Add twist of Lemon Peel and drop in glass.

BOLERO COCKTAIL

1 1/2 oz. Old Mr. Boston Imported
        Rum
    3/4 oz. Applejack
    1/4 Teaspoon Italian Vermouth
Shake well with cracked Ice and strain into 3 oz. Cocktail glass.

B

BOLO COCKTAIL

2 oz. Old Mr. Boston Imported Rum
Juice of 1/2 Lime
Juice of 1/4 Orange
1 Teaspoon Powdered Sugar
Stir well with cracked Ice and strain
into 4 oz. Cocktail glass.

**BOMBAY
COCKTAIL**

1/2 oz. French Vermouth
1/2 oz. Italian Vermouth
1 oz. Old Mr. Boston California
Brandy
1/4 Teaspoon Absinthe substitute
1/2 Teaspoon Old Mr. Boston
Curacao
Shake well with cracked Ice and strain
into 3 oz. Cocktail glass.

BOMBAY PUNCH

Juice of 1 Dozen Lemons
Add enough Powdered Sugar to
Sweeten
Place large block of Ice in Punch
bowl and stir. Then add:
1 qt. Old Mr. Boston California
Brandy
1 qt. Sherry Wine
1/4 pt. Maraschino
1/4 pt. Old Mr. Boston Curacao
4 qts. Champagne
2 qts. Carbonated Water
Some prefer to add the strained contents of a Pot of Tea. Stir well and
decorate with fruits in season. Serve
in 4 oz. Punch glasses.

**BOOSTER
COCKTAIL**

1 Teaspoon Old Mr. Boston Curacao
White of 1 Egg
2 oz. Old Mr. Boston California
Brandy
Shake well with cracked Ice and strain
into 4 oz. Cocktail glass. Grate Nutmeg on top.

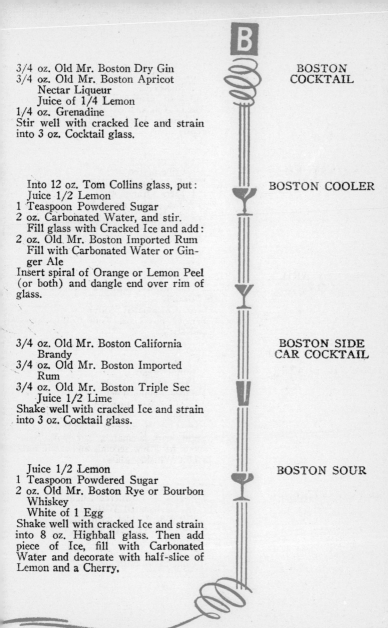

BOSTON COCKTAIL

3/4 oz. Old Mr. Boston Dry Gin
3/4 oz. Old Mr. Boston Apricot
    Nectar Liqueur
    Juice of 1/4 Lemon
1/4 oz. Grenadine
Stir well with cracked Ice and strain
into 3 oz. Cocktail glass.

BOSTON COOLER

Into 12 oz. Tom Collins glass, put:
    Juice 1/2 Lemon
1 Teaspoon Powdered Sugar
2 oz. Carbonated Water, and stir.
Fill glass with Cracked Ice and add:
2 oz. Old Mr. Boston Imported Rum
    Fill with Carbonated Water or Gin-
    ger Ale
Insert spiral of Orange or Lemon Peel
(or both) and dangle end over rim of
glass.

BOSTON SIDE CAR COCKTAIL

3/4 oz. Old Mr. Boston California
    Brandy
3/4 oz. Old Mr. Boston Imported
    Rum
3/4 oz. Old Mr. Boston Triple Sec
    Juice 1/2 Lime
Shake well with cracked Ice and strain
into 3 oz. Cocktail glass.

BOSTON SOUR

    Juice 1/2 Lemon
1 Teaspoon Powdered Sugar
2 oz. Old Mr. Boston Rye or Bourbon
    Whiskey
    White of 1 Egg
Shake well with cracked Ice and strain
into 8 oz. Highball glass. Then add
piece of Ice, fill with Carbonated
Water and decorate with half-slice of
Lemon and a Cherry.

B

BOURBON HIGHBALL

1 Cube of Ice
2 oz. Old Mr. Boston Bourbon
   Whiskey
Fill 8 oz. Highball glass with Ginger
Ale or Carbonated Water. Add twist
of Lemon Peel, if desired, and stir
gently.

BRAINSTORM COCKTAIL

   Cube of Ice
1/2 Teaspoon Benedictine
  1 Piece Orange Peel
1/2 Teaspoon French Vermouth
  2 oz. Irish Whiskey
Serve with a small bar spoon. Use
Old Fashioned Cocktail glass and stir.

BRANDY AND SODA

2 Cubes of Ice
2 oz. Old Mr. Boston California
   Brandy
6 oz. Carbonated Water
Service in 12 oz. Tom Collins glass
and stir.

BRANDY BLAZER

1 Lump Sugar
1 Piece Orange Peel
1 Piece Lemon Peel
2 oz. Old Mr. Boston California
   Brandy
Use Old Fashioned Cocktail glass.
Light with a match, stir with long
spoon for a few seconds and strain into
a Hot Whiskey glass.

BRANDY COBBLER

1 Teaspoon Powdered Sugar
2 oz. Carbonated Water
   Fill 8 oz. Goblet with Shaved Ice
   Add 2 oz. Old Mr. Boston California
   Brandy
Stir well and decorate with fruits in
season. Serve with straws.

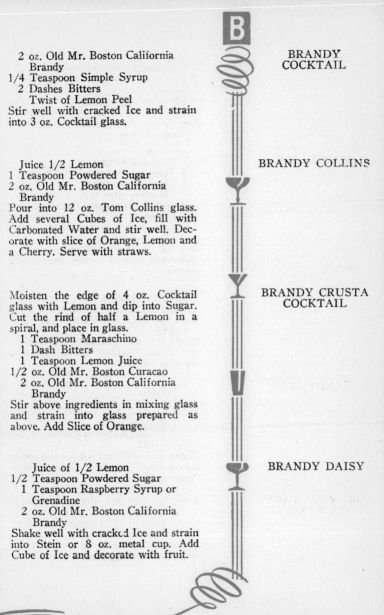

BRANDY COCKTAIL

2 oz. Old **Mr.** Boston California
   Brandy
1/4 Teaspoon Simple Syrup
2 Dashes Bitters
   Twist of Lemon Peel
Stir well with cracked Ice and strain
into 3 oz. Cocktail glass.

BRANDY COLLINS

Juice 1/2 Lemon
1 Teaspoon Powdered Sugar
2 oz. Old Mr. Boston California
   Brandy
Pour into 12 oz. Tom Collins glass.
Add several Cubes of Ice, fill with
Carbonated Water and stir well. Decorate with slice of Orange, Lemon and
a Cherry. Serve with straws.

BRANDY CRUSTA COCKTAIL

Moisten the edge of 4 oz. Cocktail
glass with Lemon and dip into Sugar.
Cut the rind of half a Lemon in a
spiral, and place in glass.
   1 Teaspoon Maraschino
   1 Dash Bitters
   1 Teaspoon Lemon Juice
1/2 oz. Old Mr. Boston Curacao
  2 oz. Old Mr. Boston California
   Brandy
Stir above ingredients in mixing glass
and strain into glass prepared as
above. Add Slice of Orange.

BRANDY DAISY

Juice of 1/2 Lemon
1/2 Teaspoon Powdered Sugar
  1 Teaspoon Raspberry Syrup or
   Grenadine
  2 oz. Old Mr. Boston California
   Brandy
Shake well with cracked Ice and strain
into Stein or 8 oz. metal cup. Add
Cube of Ice and decorate with fruit.

33

B

BRANDY EGG NOGG

1 Egg
1 Teaspoon Powdered Sugar
2 oz. Old Mr. Boston California Brandy
Fill glass with Milk

Shake well with cracked Ice and strain into 12 oz. Tom Collins glass. Grate Nutmeg on top.

BRANDY FIX

Juice 1/2 Lemon
1 Teaspoon Powdered Sugar
1 Teaspoon Water and stir
Fill glass with Shaved Ice
2 oz. Old Mr. Boston California Brandy
1/2 oz. Old Mr. Boston Wild Cherry Flavored Brandy

Use 12 oz. Tom Collins glass. Stir well. Add slice of Lemon. Serve with straws.

BRANDY FIZZ

Juice 1/2 Lemon
1 Teaspoon Powdered Sugar
2 oz. Old Mr. Boston California Brandy

Shake well with cracked Ice and strain into 7 oz. Highball glass. Fill with Carbonated Water.

BRANDY FLIP

1 Egg
1 Teaspoon Powdered Sugar
1 1/2 oz. Old Mr. Boston California Brandy
2 Teaspoons Sweet Cream (if desired)

Shake well with cracked Ice and strain into 4 oz. Flip glass. Grate a little Nutmeg on top.

BRANDY GUMP COCKTAIL

1 1/2 oz. Old Mr. Boston California Brandy
Juice of 1/2 Lemon
1/2 Teaspoon Grenadine

Shake well with cracked Ice and strain into 3 oz. Cocktail glass.

1 Cube of Ice
2 oz. Old Mr. Boston California
  Brandy
Fill 8 oz. Highball glass with Ginger
Ale or Carbonated Water. Add twist
of Lemon Peel, if desired, and stir
gently.

BRANDY HIGHBALL

Into 12 oz. Tom Collins glass put:
1 Teaspoon Powdered Sugar
5 or 6 Sprigs Fresh Mint
2 oz. Old Mr. Boston California
  Brandy
1 oz. Old Mr. Boston Peach Flavored
  Brandy
Then fill glass with finely shaved Ice,
and stir until Mint rises to top, being
careful not to bruise Mint. (Do not
hold glass with hand while stirring.)
Decorate with slice of Pineapple,
Orange, Lemon and a Cherry. Serve
with straws.

BRANDY JULEP

1 Teaspoon Powdered Sugar
2 oz. Old Mr. Boston California
  Brandy
1/2 Pint Milk
Shake well with cracked Ice, strain
into 12 oz. Tom Collins glass and
grate Nutmeg on top.

BRANDY MILK PUNCH

Juice of 1 Dozen Lemons
Juice of 4 Oranges
Add enough Sugar to sweeten
8 oz. Grenadine
1 qt. Carbonated Water
Place large block of Ice in Punch
Bowl and stir well. Then add:
1/2 Pint Old Mr. Boston Curacao
2 qts. Old Mr. Boston California
  Brandy
Some prefer to add the strained contents of a Pot of Tea. Stir well and
decorate with fruits in season. Serve
in 4 oz. Punch glasses.

BRANDY PUNCH

B

BRANDY SANGAREE

1 1/2 oz. Old Mr. Boston California
    Brandy
   1 Teaspoon Powdered Sugar
Shake well with cracked Ice and strain
into 3 oz. Cocktail glass, leaving
enough room in which to float a Tablespoon of Port Wine.

BRANDY SLING

Dissolve 1 Teaspoon Powdered Sugar
in Teaspoon of Water.
2 oz. Old Mr. Boston California
    Brandy
2 Cubes of Ice
Serve in Old Fashioned Cocktail glass
and stir. Twist of Lemon Peel and
drop in glass.

BRANDY SMASH

Muddle 1 Lump of Sugar with
1 oz. Carbonated Water and
4 Sprigs of Green Mint
Add 2 oz. Old Mr. Boston California
Brandy, then a Cube of Ice. Stir and
decorate with a slice of Orange and a
Cherry. Twist Lemon Peel on top. Use
Old Fashioned Cocktail glass.

BRANDY SOUR

Juice 1/2 Lemon
1/2 Teaspoon Powdered Sugar
  2 oz. Old Mr. Boston California
    Brandy
Shake well with cracked Ice and strain
into 6 oz. Sour glass. Fill with Carbonated Water. Decorate with a half-
slice of Lemon and a Cherry.

BRANDY SQUIRT

1 1/2 oz. Old Mr. Boston California
    Brandy
   1 Tablespoon Powdered Sugar
   1 Teaspoon Raspberry Syrup or
    Grenadine
Stir well with cracked Ice and strain
into 8 oz. Highball glass and fill with
Carbonated Water. Decorate with
Cubes of Pineapple and Strawberries.

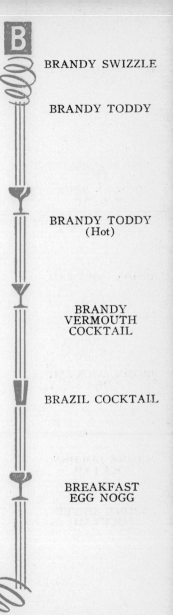

BRANDY SWIZZLE

Made same as Gin Swizzle, using 2 oz. Old Mr. Boston California Brandy.

BRANDY TODDY

Use Old Fashioned Cocktail glass.
1/2 Teaspoon Powdered Sugar
  2 Teaspoons Water
  2 oz. Old Mr. Boston California
    Brandy
  1 Lump of Ice
Stir well and Twist Lemon Peel on top.

BRANDY TODDY (Hot)

Put lump of Sugar into Hot Whiskey glass and fill with two-thirds Boiling Water. Add 2 oz. Old Mr. Boston California Brandy. Stir and decorate with Slice of Lemon. Grate Nutmeg on top.

BRANDY VERMOUTH COCKTAIL

1/2 oz. Italian Vermouth
  2 oz. Old Mr. Boston California
    Brandy
  1 Dash Bitters
Stir well with cracked Ice and strain into 3 oz. Cocktail glass.

BRAZIL COCKTAIL

1 1/4 oz. French Vermouth
1 1/4 oz. Sherry Wine
    1 Dash Bitters
    1/4 Teaspoon Absinthe substitute
Stir well with cracked Ice and strain into 3 oz. Cocktail glass.

BREAKFAST EGG NOGG

  1 Egg
1/2 oz. Old Mr. Boston Curacao
  2 oz. Old Mr. Boston Apricot Flavored Brandy
    Fill glass with Milk
Shake well with cracked Ice and strain into 12 oz. Tom Collins glass. Grate Nutmeg on top.

BRIGHTON PUNCH

3/4 oz. Old Mr. Boston Rye or Bourbon Whiskey
3/4 oz. Cognac
3/4 oz. Benedictine
Juice 1/2 Orange
Juice 1/2 Lemon
Fill 12 oz. Tom Collins glass with shaved Ice and Carbonated Water and stir. Serve with straws.

BROKEN SPUR COCKTAIL

3/4 oz. Italian Vermouth
1 1/2 oz. Port Wine
1/4 Teaspoon Old Mr. Boston Curacao
Shake well with cracked Ice and strain into 3 oz. Cocktail glass.

BRONX COCKTAIL

1 oz. Old Mr. Boston Dry Gin
1/2 oz. French Vermouth
1/2 oz. Italian Vermouth
Twist of Orange Peel
Shake well with cracked Ice and strain into 3 oz. Cocktail glass. Serve with Slice of Orange.

BRONX COCKTAIL (Dry)

1 oz. Old Mr. Boston Dry Gin
1 oz. French Vermouth
Twist of Orange Peel
Shake well with cracked Ice and strain into 3 oz. Cocktail glass. Serve with Slice of Orange.

BRONX GOLDEN COCKTAIL

Made same as Bronx Cocktail, adding the Yolk of one Egg. Use 4 oz. Cocktail glass.

BRONX SILVER COCKTAIL

Juice of 1/4 Orange
White of 1 Egg
1/2 oz. French Vermouth
1 oz. Old Mr. Boston Dry Gin
Shake well with cracked Ice and strain into 4 oz. Cocktail glass.

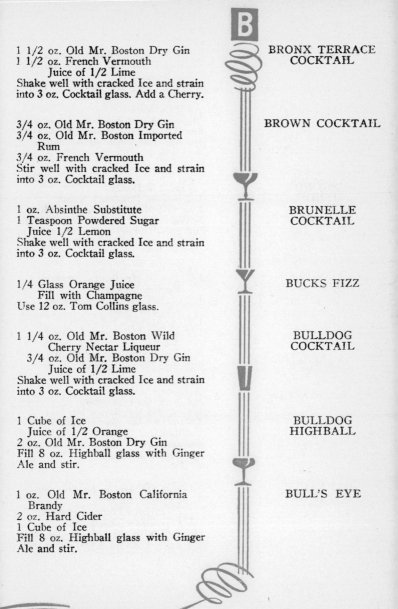

B

1 1/2 oz. Old Mr. Boston Dry Gin
1 1/2 oz. French Vermouth
    Juice of 1/2 Lime
Shake well with cracked Ice and strain
into 3 oz. Cocktail glass. Add a Cherry.

**BRONX TERRACE
COCKTAIL**

3/4 oz. Old Mr. Boston Dry Gin
3/4 oz. Old Mr. Boston Imported
    Rum
3/4 oz. French Vermouth
Stir well with cracked Ice and strain
into 3 oz. Cocktail glass.

BROWN COCKTAIL

1 oz. Absinthe Substitute
1 Teaspoon Powdered Sugar
    Juice 1/2 Lemon
Shake well with cracked Ice and strain
into 3 oz. Cocktail glass.

**BRUNELLE
COCKTAIL**

1/4 Glass Orange Juice
    Fill with Champagne
Use 12 oz. Tom Collins glass.

BUCKS FIZZ

1 1/4 oz. Old Mr. Boston Wild
    Cherry Nectar Liqueur
  3/4 oz. Old Mr. Boston Dry Gin
    Juice of 1/2 Lime
Shake well with cracked Ice and strain
into 3 oz. Cocktail glass.

**BULLDOG
COCKTAIL**

1 Cube of Ice
    Juice of 1/2 Orange
2 oz. Old Mr. Boston Dry Gin
Fill 8 oz. Highball glass with Ginger
Ale and stir.

**BULLDOG
HIGHBALL**

1 oz. Old Mr. Boston California
    Brandy
2 oz. Hard Cider
1 Cube of Ice
Fill 8 oz. Highball glass with Ginger
Ale and stir.

BULL'S EYE

BULL'S MILK

1 Teaspoon Powdered Sugar
1 oz. Old Mr. Boston Imported Rum
1 1/2 oz. Old Mr. Boston California Brandy
1/2 pt. Milk

Shake well with cracked Ice and strain into 12 oz. Tom Collins glass. Grate Nutmeg and pinch of Cinnamon on top.

BURGUNDY BISHOP

Juice 1/4 Lemon
1 Teaspoon Powdered Sugar
1 oz. Old Mr. Boston Imported Rum

Shake well and strain into 8 oz. Highball glass and fill with Burgundy and stir. Decorate with Fruits.

BUTTON HOOK COCKTAIL

1/2 oz. Old Mr. Boston Creme de Menthe (White)
1/2 oz. Old Mr. Boston Apricot Flavored Brandy
1/2 oz. Absinthe Substitute
1/2 oz. Old Mr. Boston California Brandy

Shake well with cracked Ice and strain into 3 oz. Cocktail glass.

B. V. D. COCKTAIL

3/4 oz. French Vermouth
3/4 oz. Old Mr. Boston Dry Gin
3/4 oz. Old Mr. Boston Imported Rum

Stir well with cracked Ice and strain into 3 oz. Cocktail glass.

CABARET COCKTAIL

1 1/2 oz. Old Mr. Boston Dry Gin
2 Dashes Bitters
1/2 Teaspoon French Vermouth
1/4 Teaspoon Benedictine

Stir well with cracked Ice and strain into 3 oz. Cocktail glass. Serve with a Cherry.

Juice 1/2 Lemon
1 Teaspoon Powdered Sugar
2 oz. Old Mr. Boston Rye or Bourbon
   Whiskey
Stir well with cracked Ice and fill with
Ginger Ale. Use 8 oz. Highball glass.

CABLEGRAM HIGHBALL

White of 1 Egg
1 Teaspoon Absinthe Substitute
1 Teaspoon Sweet Cream
1 1/2 oz. Old Mr. Boston Dry Gin
Shake well with cracked Ice and strain
into 4 oz. Cocktail glass.

CAFE DE PARIS COCKTAIL

1 Cup Hot Black Coffee
Put Cube of Sugar, well soaked with
Old Mr. Boston California Brandy,
in teaspoon and hold so that it will
rest on top of coffee and ignite and hold
until flame burns out. Drop contents
in Coffee.

CAFE ROYAL

Juice 1 Lemon
Juice 1 Lime
3 Teaspoons Powdered Sugar
2 oz. Old Mr. Boston Rye or
   Bourbon Whiskey
1/4 Teaspoon Grenadine
Shake well with cracked Ice and strain
into 12 oz. Tom Collins glass filled
with Shaved Ice. Fill with Carbonated
Water and decorate with slice of
Orange, Lemon and a Cherry. Serve
with straws.

CALIFORNIA LEMONADE

3/4 oz. Scotch Whiskey
3/4 oz. Irish Whiskey
Juice 1/4 Lemon
2 Dashes Orange Bitters
Shake well with cracked Ice and strain
into 3 oz. Cocktail glass.

CAMERON'S KICK COCKTAIL

CARDINAL PUNCH

Juice of 1 Dozen Lemons
Add enough Powdered Sugar to sweeten
1 qt. Carbonated Water
Place large block of Ice in Punch Bowl and stir well. Then add:
2 qts. Claret
1 pt. Old Mr. Boston California Brandy
1 pt. Old Mr. Boston Imported Rum
1 pt. Champagne
1/2 pt. Italian Vermouth

Some prefer to add the strained contents of a Pot of Tea. Stir well and decorate with fruits in season. Serve in 4 oz. Punch glasses.

CARROL COCKTAIL

1 1/2 oz. Old Mr. Boston California Brandy
3/4 oz. Italian Vermouth

Stir well with cracked Ice and strain into 3 oz. Cocktail glass. Serve with a Cherry.

CARUSO COCKTAIL

3/4 oz. Old Mr. Boston Dry Gin
3/4 oz. French Vermouth
3/4 oz. Old Mr. Boston Creme de Menthe (Green)

Stir well with cracked Ice and strain into 3 oz. Cocktail glass.

CASCADE

1 oz. French Vermouth
1 oz. Creme de Cassis
1 Cube of Ice

Use 8 oz. Stem Goblet and fill balance with Carbonated Water and stir.

CASINO COCKTAIL

2 Dashes Orange Bitters
1/4 Teaspoon Maraschino
1/4 Teaspoon Lemon Juice
2 oz. Old Mr. Boston Dry Gin

Shake well with cracked Ice and strain into 3 oz. Cocktail glass. Serve with a Cherry.

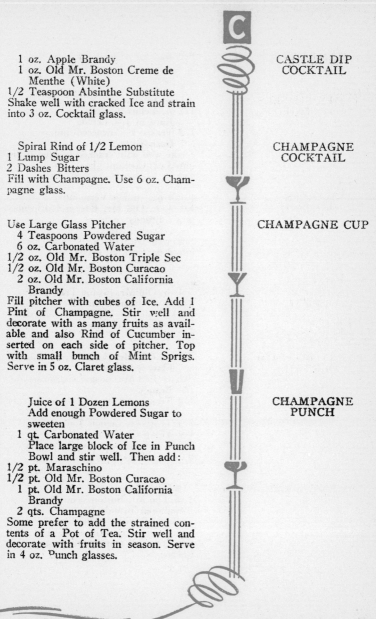

1 oz. Apple Brandy
1 oz. Old Mr. Boston Creme de
   Menthe (White)
1/2 Teaspoon Absinthe Substitute
Shake well with cracked Ice and strain
into 3 oz. Cocktail glass.

CASTLE DIP COCKTAIL

Spiral Rind of 1/2 Lemon
1 Lump Sugar
2 Dashes Bitters
Fill with Champagne. Use 6 oz. Champagne glass.

CHAMPAGNE COCKTAIL

Use Large Glass Pitcher
   4 Teaspoons Powdered Sugar
   6 oz. Carbonated Water
1/2 oz. Old Mr. Boston Triple Sec
1/2 oz. Old Mr. Boston Curacao
   2 oz. Old Mr. Boston California
      Brandy
Fill pitcher with cubes of Ice. Add 1
Pint of Champagne. Stir well and
decorate with as many fruits as available and also Rind of Cucumber inserted on each side of pitcher. Top
with small bunch of Mint Sprigs.
Serve in 5 oz. Claret glass.

CHAMPAGNE CUP

Juice of 1 Dozen Lemons
   Add enough Powdered Sugar to
   sweeten
1 qt. Carbonated Water
   Place large block of Ice in Punch
   Bowl and stir well. Then add:
1/2 pt. Maraschino
1/2 pt. Old Mr. Boston Curacao
   1 pt. Old Mr. Boston California
      Brandy
   2 qts. Champagne
Some prefer to add the strained contents of a Pot of Tea. Stir well and
decorate with fruits in season. Serve
in 4 oz. Punch glasses.

CHAMPAGNE PUNCH

43

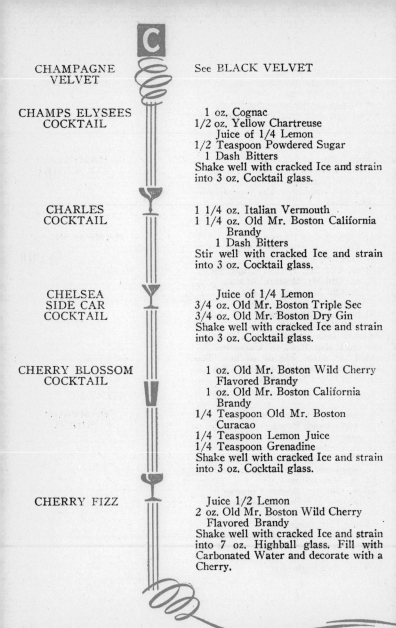

C

CHAMPAGNE
VELVET

See BLACK VELVET

CHAMPS ELYSEES
COCKTAIL

1 oz. Cognac
1/2 oz. Yellow Chartreuse
Juice of 1/4 Lemon
1/2 Teaspoon Powdered Sugar
1 Dash Bitters
Shake well with cracked Ice and strain
into 3 oz. Cocktail glass.

CHARLES
COCKTAIL

1 1/4 oz. Italian Vermouth
1 1/4 oz. Old Mr. Boston California
Brandy
1 Dash Bitters
Stir well with cracked Ice and strain
into 3 oz. Cocktail glass.

CHELSEA
SIDE CAR
COCKTAIL

Juice of 1/4 Lemon
3/4 oz. Old Mr. Boston Triple Sec
3/4 oz. Old Mr. Boston Dry Gin
Shake well with cracked Ice and strain
into 3 oz. Cocktail glass.

CHERRY BLOSSOM
COCKTAIL

1 oz. Old Mr. Boston Wild Cherry
Flavored Brandy
1 oz. Old Mr. Boston California
Brandy
1/4 Teaspoon Old Mr. Boston
Curacao
1/4 Teaspoon Lemon Juice
1/4 Teaspoon Grenadine
Shake well with cracked Ice and strain
into 3 oz. Cocktail glass.

CHERRY FIZZ

Juice 1/2 Lemon
2 oz. Old Mr. Boston Wild Cherry
Flavored Brandy
Shake well with cracked Ice and strain
into 7 oz. Highball glass. Fill with
Carbonated Water and decorate with a
Cherry.

1 Egg
1 Teaspoon Powdered Sugar
1 1/2 oz. Old Mr. Boston Wild Cherry
    Flavored Brandy
2 Teaspoons Sweet Cream (if
    desired)
Shake well with cracked Ice and strain
into 4 oz. Flip glass. Grate a little
Nutmeg on top.

CHERRY FLIP

2 Cubes of Ice
1 oz. Old Mr. Boston Wild Cherry
    Flavored Brandy
1 oz. Old Mr. Boston Dry Gin
Serve in Old Fashioned Cocktail glass
and stir. Twist of Lemon Peel and
drop in glass.

CHERRY SLING

2 oz. Old Mr. Boston California
    Brandy
1 Dash Bitters
1/4 Teaspoon Old Mr. Boston
    Curacao
Shake well with cracked Ice and strain
into Champagne glass. Frost glass by
rubbing slice of Lemon around rim
and then dip in Powdered Sugar.

**CHICAGO
COCKTAIL**

Juice 1/2 Lemon
1 Teaspoon Powdered Sugar
    White of 1 Egg
1 oz. Port Wine
1 oz. Old Mr. Boston Imported Rum
Shake well with cracked Ice and strain
into 7 oz. Highball glass. Fill with
Carbonated Water.

CHICAGO FIZZ

1/2 oz. Grenadine
1 1/2 oz. Jamaica Rum
    1 Dash Bitters
    1 Teaspoon Maraschino
    1 Teaspoon Old Mr. Boston
      Curacao
Shake well with cracked Ice and strain
into 3 oz. Cocktail glass.

**CHINESE
COCKTAIL**

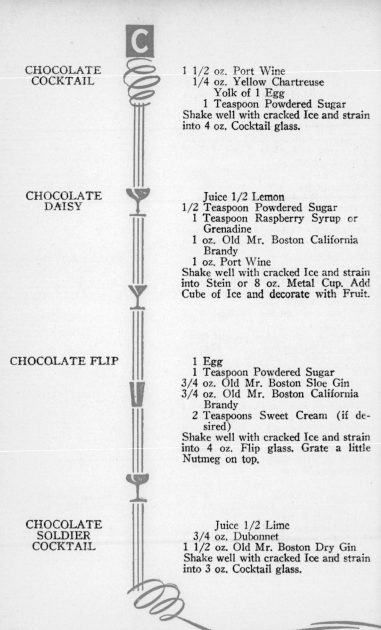

CHOCOLATE COCKTAIL

1 1/2 oz. Port Wine
1/4 oz. Yellow Chartreuse
Yolk of 1 Egg
1 Teaspoon Powdered Sugar
Shake well with cracked Ice and strain into 4 oz. Cocktail glass.

CHOCOLATE DAISY

Juice 1/2 Lemon
1/2 Teaspoon Powdered Sugar
1 Teaspoon Raspberry Syrup or Grenadine
1 oz. Old Mr. Boston California Brandy
1 oz. Port Wine
Shake well with cracked Ice and strain into Stein or 8 oz. Metal Cup. Add Cube of Ice and decorate with Fruit.

CHOCOLATE FLIP

1 Egg
1 Teaspoon Powdered Sugar
3/4 oz. Old Mr. Boston Sloe Gin
3/4 oz. Old Mr. Boston California Brandy
2 Teaspoons Sweet Cream (if desired)
Shake well with cracked Ice and strain into 4 oz. Flip glass. Grate a little Nutmeg on top.

CHOCOLATE SOLDIER COCKTAIL

Juice 1/2 Lime
3/4 oz. Dubonnet
1 1/2 oz. Old Mr. Boston Dry Gin
Shake well with cracked Ice and strain into 3 oz. Cocktail glass.

Beat the yolks and whites of 1 Dozen Eggs separately and then pour together and add:

1 Pinch Baking Soda
6 oz. Old Mr. Boston Imported Rum
2 lbs. Granulated Sugar
and then beat into stiff batter. Then add:
1 qt. Milk
1 qt. Sweet Cream
2 qts. Old Mr. Boston Rye or Bourbon Whiskey and stir. Set in refrigerator over night.

Before serving, stir again, and serve in 4 oz. Punch glasses, and grate Nutmeg on top.

CHRISTMAS YULE EGG NOGG

1 oz. Benedictine
1 oz. French Vermouth
1 Teaspoon Absinthe Substitute
Shake well with cracked Ice and strain into 3 oz. Cocktail glass.

CHRYSANTHEMUM COCKTAIL

Use Large Glass Pitcher
4 Teaspoons Powdered Sugar
6 oz. Carbonated Water
1/2 oz. Old Mr. Boston Triple Sec
1/2 oz. Old Mr. Boston Curacao
2 oz. Old Mr. Boston California Brandy
Fill pitcher with cubes of Ice. Add 1 Pint of Cider. Stir well and decorate with as many Fruits as available and also Rind of Cucumber inserted on each side of pitcher. Top with small bunch of Mint Sprigs. Serve in 5 oz. Claret glass.

CIDER CUP

1 Egg
1 Teaspoon Powdered Sugar
1/4 pt. Milk
Shake well with cracked Ice and strain into 12 oz. Tom Collins glass. Then fill glass with Sweet Cider. Grate Nutmeg on top.

CIDER EGG NOGG

C

CIRCUS RICKEY

1 Cube of Ice
Juice 1/2 Lime
1/2 Teaspoon Grenadine
1 1/2 oz. Old Mr. Boston Dry Gin
Fill 8 oz. Highball glass with Carbonated Water and stir. Leave Lime in glass.

CLARET COBBLER

1 Teaspoon Powdered Sugar
2 oz. Carbonated Water and stir
Fill 8 oz. Goblet with Shaved Ice and float 3 oz. Claret on top
Decorate with fruits in season. Serve with straws.

CLARET CUP

Use Large Glass Pitcher
4 Teaspoons Powdered Sugar
6 oz. Carbonated Water
1/2 oz. Old Mr. Boston Triple Sec
1/2 oz. Old Mr. Boston Curacao
2 oz. Old Mr. Boston California Brandy
Fill pitcher with cubes of Ice. Add 1 Pint of Claret. Stir well and decorate with as many fruits as available and also Rind of Cucumber inserted on each side of pitcher. Top with small bunch of Mint Sprigs. Serve in 5 oz. Claret glass.

CLARET PUNCH

Juice of 1 Dozen Lemons
Add enough Powdered Sugar to sweeten
1 qt. Carbonated Water
Place large block of Ice in Punch Bowl and stir well. Then add:
1/2 pt. Old Mr. Boston Curacao
1 pt. Old Mr. Boston California Brandy
3 qts. Claret
Some prefer to add the strained contents of a Pot of Tea. Stir well and decorate with fruits in season. Serve in 4 oz. Punch glasses.

Fine Liquors In The Old Boston Tradition

Sirs —

May I have the honor to present for your approval and pleasure my illustrious family of fine liquors . . . liquors steeped in the traditions of old Boston.

And proud may they be of their glorious kinship. For each and every bottle truly reflects the sterling character and skilled craftsmanship that for three centuries have been honored traditions of my city.

Gentlemen, from the shadows of Bunker Hill, Faneuil Hall, the Old South Church — inspiring monuments all to this eternal spirit — I offer, for the consummation of your pleasure, my distinguished line of liquors.

Mr. Boston

Old State House — 1748
In this historic structure John Hancock, the first governor of Massachusetts was inaugurated in 1780.

FANCIERS of rare bourbon will prize the robust flavor of this fine old whiskey. Five long years ago, it was stored in scientifically heated warehouses to age and mellow — to acquire the rich character it so abundantly possesses.

Also available in Rye — 86 proof

The Old Bridge At Concord — 1775

"By the rude bridge that arched the flood,
Their flag to April's breeze unfurled,
Here once the embattled farmers stood
And fired the shot heard 'round the world."

ONE taste will reveal why Pinch Bottle has been rightfully acclaimed masterpiece of all blended whiskies. For here is a golden amber whiskey — as distinctive in character as its bottle is distinguished in appearance. Serve Pinch Bottle with pride!

72½% grain neutral spirits — 86 Proof

THOSE who lean toward lighter whiskey will welcome the Scotch-like mildness of this delicate bourbon. Like bottled in bond, it has enjoyed a long, four year slumber in charred oak casks — but it offers the extra mildness of a gentler 85 proof.

This whiskey is 4 years old

Faneuil Hall

In Colonial times, the "Cradle of Liberty" was the scene of many stirring meetings and historical events.

OLD sailing captains, retired from the sea, often lashed a keg of whiskey under their rocking chairs. Thus, they duplicated the rolling motion of sailing ships which gave their whiskey finer flavor. Mr. Boston recaptures that flavor in Rocking Chair.

75% grain neutral spirits—85 Proof

Old North Church
On the night of April 18, 1775, signal lanterns hung in this famous steeple, warned of the approaching British.

17 rare flavors—*all imported*—are skillfully blended to give this gin its matchless flavor and bouquet. Cardamon, coriander, lovage root, cloves — to name a few — achieve a deep taste difference found in Old Mr. Boston Dry Gin alone.

Distilled from 100% grain neutral spirits—90 Proof

FROM plum-like, imported sloe berries comes the refreshing Burgundy flavor in Old Mr. Boston Sloe Gin. Taste its tempting, wine-like tang, and you'll discover why it's *America's largest selling Sloe Gin* — regardless of price!

70 Proof

Old South Church

Constructed in 1729, this towering edifice was the Colonial meeting place of many inspired historical gatherings.

OFTEN called bottled sunshine — here is the delightful taste-tempter that greets you with the refreshing flavor of juicy, sun-kissed oranges. Give your taste a fresh, sunny view on life — introduce it to this luscious liquor.

70 Proof

IMAGINE, if you will, an emerald-hued, satin smooth liquor—gently yielding the crisp, cooling fragrance of dew-drenched mint! In a refreshing *Mint Collins*, or even straight, you'll find this appealing drink a taste treat you'll long remember.

70 Proof

HONEY smooth yet rich as old brandy— that's delicious Apricot Nectar! In every drop of this hearty liquor, you can taste the luscious flavor of fresh-picked apricots. Three other delicious Nectars, too — *Blackberry, Peach, Wild Cherry.*

70 Proof

IN the far-off Virgin Islands basks the birthplace of this Rum . . . imported, yet *duty free!* It's light in character, bright in color. Makes a Cuba Libre, Rum Collins or Daiquiri soothing as silver-twilight on a palm-fringed isle.

Also Imported Dark Rum

86 Proof

CLUSTERS of ripened grapes, flushed with the summer's sun, have generously imparted to this fine brandy a sweet richness and delicate flavor which brings to mind Old World brandies of rare distinction. *86 Proof.*

Also Apricot, Blackberry, Peach, Wild Cherry flavored Brandies
70 Proof

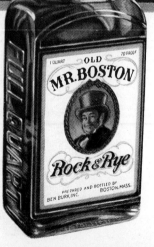

COME sleet, come snow — here's America's traditional Rock & Rye, comforting as a crackling fire. The *Clearfruit Process* preserves the crisp freshness of the floating fruit. This old standby almost makes midwinter seem like May!

70 Proof

1 QUART — OLD — 70 PROOF
MR. BOSTON
Rock & Rye
PREPARED AND BOTTLED BY
BEN BURK, INC. — BOSTON, MASS.

FULL QUART

The Lamb Tavern
In the winter of 1697, from the "Sign of the Lamb," the first stage coach left Boston on the newly opened run to Providence.

CHOICE whiskey is artfully blended with satin-smooth liqueur to produce this delightful miracle of mildness. *"Drink it straight—needs no chaser"*, invitingly says its label. And grateful whiskey drinkers *do!*

70 Proof

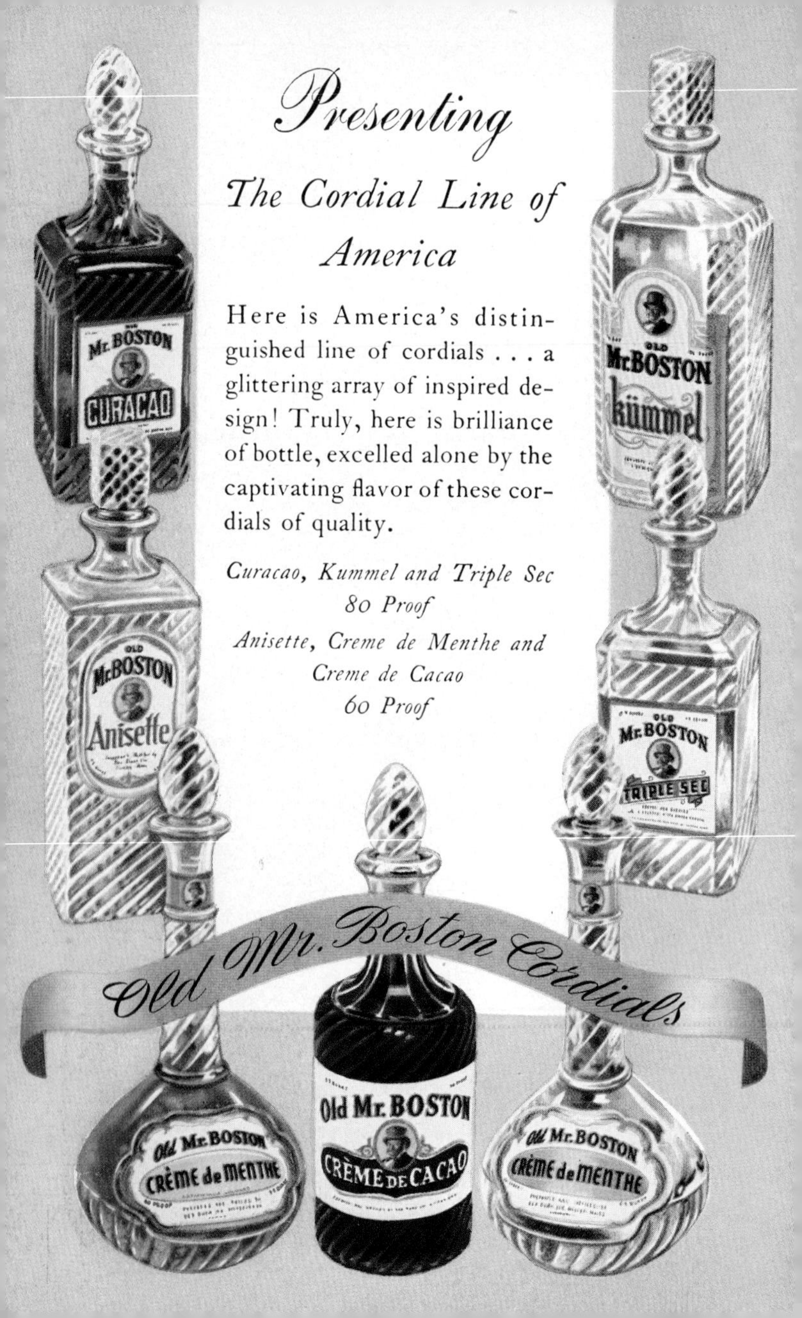

Presenting
The Cordial Line of America
Here is America's distinguished line of cordials . . . a glittering array of inspired design! Truly, here is brilliance of bottle, excelled alone by the captivating flavor of these cordials of quality.
Curacao, Kummel and Triple Sec
80 Proof
Anisette, Creme de Menthe and Creme de Cacao
60 Proof
Old Mr. Boston Cordials
Mr. BOSTON
CURACAO
OLD
Mr.BOSTON
kümmel
OLD
Mr.BOSTON
Anisette
OLD
Mr.BOSTON
TRIPLE SEC
Old Mr.BOSTON
CRÈME de MENTHE
Old Mr.BOSTON
CRÈME DE CACAO
Old Mr.BOSTON
CRÈME de MENTHE

3/4 oz. Old Mr. Boston Dry Gin
3/4 oz. French Vermouth
1/2 oz. Old Mr. Boston Apricot Flavored Brandy
1/2 oz. Old Mr. Boston Triple Sec
Stir well with cracked Ice and strain into 3 oz. Cocktail glass.

CLARIDGE COCKTAIL

Juice of 1/4 Lemon
1/4 oz. Old Mr. Boston Curacao
1/4 oz. Maraschino
1 oz. Old Mr. Boston California Brandy
Shake well with cracked Ice and strain into 3 oz. Cocktail glass. Frost rim of glass by rubbing with Lemon and dipping in Powdered Sugar.

CLASSIC COCKTAIL

1 oz. Italian Vermouth
1/2 oz. Old Mr. Boston Sloe Gin
1/2 oz. Muscatel Wine
Shake well with cracked Ice and strain into 3 oz. Cocktail glass.

CLOVE COCKTAIL

Juice 1/2 Lemon
2 Teaspoons Grenadine
White of 1 Egg
1 1/2 oz. Old Mr. Boston Dry Gin
Shake well with cracked Ice and strain into 4 oz. Cocktail glass.

CLOVER CLUB COCKTAIL

Juice 1 Lime
2 Teaspoons Grenadine
White of 1 Egg
1 1/2 oz. Old Mr. Boston Dry Gin
Shake well with cracked Ice and strain into 4 oz. Cocktail glass. Serve with Mint Leaf on top.

CLOVER LEAF COCKTAIL

1 1/2 oz. Old Mr. Boston Dry Gin
3/4 oz. Italian Vermouth
Stir well with cracked Ice and strain into 3 oz. Cocktail glass. Add a Cherry or Olive.

CLUB COCKTAIL

COBBLERS

See Index on page 5 for complete list of Cobbler recipes.

COFFEE COCKTAIL

1 Egg
1 Teaspoon Powdered Sugar
1 oz. Port Wine
1 oz. Old Mr. Boston California Brandy
Shake well with cracked Ice and strain into 4 oz. Cocktail glass. Grate Nutmeg on top.

COFFEE FLIP

1 Egg
1 Teaspoon Powdered Sugar
1 oz. Old Mr. Boston California Brandy
1 oz. Port Wine
2 Teaspoons Sweet Cream (if desired)
Shake well with cracked Ice and strain into 4 oz. Flip glass. Grate a little Nutmeg on top.

COGNAC HIGHBALL

1 Cube of Ice
2 oz. Cognac
Fill 8 oz. Highball glass with Ginger Ale or Carbonated Water. Add twist of Lemon Peel, if desired, and stir gently.

COLD DECK COCKTAIL

1/2 oz. Old Mr. Boston Creme de Menthe (White)
1/2 oz. Italian Vermouth
1 oz. Old Mr. Boston California Brandy
Shake well with cracked Ice and strain into 3 oz. Cocktail glass.

COLLINS

See Index on page 13 for complete list of Collins recipes.

COLONIAL COCKTAIL

1/2 oz. Grapefruit Juice
1 Teaspoon Maraschino
1 1/2 oz. Old Mr. Boston Dry Gin
Shake well with cracked Ice and strain into 3 oz. Cocktail glass. Serve with an Olive.

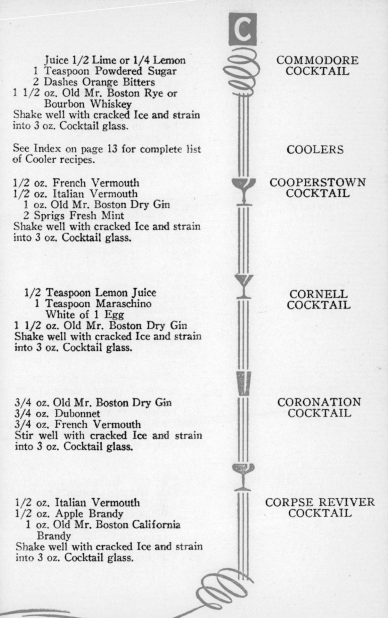

Juice 1/2 Lime or 1/4 Lemon
1 Teaspoon Powdered Sugar
2 Dashes Orange Bitters
1 1/2 oz. Old Mr. Boston Rye or
    Bourbon Whiskey
Shake well with cracked Ice and strain
into 3 oz. Cocktail glass.

COMMODORE COCKTAIL

See Index on page 13 for complete list
of Cooler recipes.

COOLERS

1/2 oz. French Vermouth
1/2 oz. Italian Vermouth
  1 oz. Old Mr. Boston Dry Gin
  2 Sprigs Fresh Mint
Shake well with cracked Ice and strain
into 3 oz. Cocktail glass.

COOPERSTOWN COCKTAIL

1/2 Teaspoon Lemon Juice
  1 Teaspoon Maraschino
    White of 1 Egg
1 1/2 oz. Old Mr. Boston Dry Gin
Shake well with cracked Ice and strain
into 3 oz. Cocktail glass.

CORNELL COCKTAIL

3/4 oz. Old Mr. Boston Dry Gin
3/4 oz. Dubonnet
3/4 oz. French Vermouth
Stir well with cracked Ice and strain
into 3 oz. Cocktail glass.

CORONATION COCKTAIL

1/2 oz. Italian Vermouth
1/2 oz. Apple Brandy
  1 oz. Old Mr. Boston California
    Brandy
Shake well with cracked Ice and strain
into 3 oz. Cocktail glass.

CORPSE REVIVER COCKTAIL

C

COUNTRY CLUB COOLER

Into 12 oz. Tom Collins glass, put:
1/2 Teaspoon Grenadine
2 oz. Carbonated Water and stir
  Fill glass with cracked Ice and add:
2 oz. French Vermouth
  Fill with Carbonated Water or Ginger Ale
Insert spiral of Orange or Lemon Peel (or both) and dangle end over rim of glass.

COWBOY COCKTAIL

1 1/2 oz. Old Mr. Boston Rye or Bourbon Whiskey
1/2 oz. Sweet Cream
Shake well with cracked Ice and strain into 3 oz. Cocktail glass.

CREAM FIZZ

Juice 1/2 Lemon
1 Teaspoon Powdered Sugar
2 oz. Old Mr. Boston Dry Gin
1 Teaspoon Fresh Cream
Shake well with cracked Ice and strain into 8 oz. Highball glass. Fill with Carbonated Water.

CREAM PUFF

2 oz. Old Mr. Boston Imported Rum
1 oz. Sweet Cream
1/2 Teaspoon Powdered Sugar
Shake well with cracked Ice and strain into 8 oz. Highball glass. Fill with Carbonated Water and stir.

CREME DE GIN COCKTAIL

1 1/2 oz. Old Mr. Boston Dry Gin
1/2 oz. Old Mr. Boston Creme de Menthe
  White of 1 Egg
2 Teaspoons Lemon Juice
2 Teaspoons Orange Juice
Shake well with cracked Ice and strain into 4 oz. Cocktail glass.

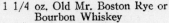

1 1/4 oz. Old Mr. Boston Rye or
　　　Bourbon Whiskey
1 1/4 oz. Madeira Wine
　　1 Teaspoon Grenadine
Stir well with cracked Ice and strain
into 3 oz. Cocktail glass. Serve with 1
Green Cherry, 1 Red Cherry and 1
White Cherry.

**CREOLE LADY
COCKTAIL**

1 1/2 oz. Old Mr. Boston Dry Gin
　　2 Teaspoons Lemon Juice
　　1 Teaspoon Grenadine
Shake well with cracked Ice and strain
into 3 oz. Cocktail glass, leaving
enough room on top to float 3/4 oz.
Port Wine.

**CRIMSON
COCKTAIL**

　　Juice of 1/4 Lemon
　1/4 Teaspoon Grenadine
1 1/2 oz. Old Mr. Boston Rye or
　　　Bourbon Whiskey
Shake well with cracked Ice and strain
into 3 oz. Cocktail glass.

CROW COCKTAIL

　1/2 oz. Creme de Yvette
　　2 Dashes Orange Bitters
1 1/2 oz. Old Mr. Boston Dry Gin
Shake well with cracked Ice and strain
into 3 oz. Cocktail glass.

**CRYSTAL SLIPPER
COCKTAIL**

　Juice 1/2 Lime—Drop skin in glass
2 oz. Old Mr. Boston Imported Rum
2 Cubes of Ice
　Fill glass with any Cola
Use 10 oz. glass and stir well.

CUBA LIBRE

　　Juice of 1/2 Lime
　1/2 Teaspoon Powdered Sugar
　　2 oz. Old Mr. Boston Imported
　　　Rum
Shake well with cracked Ice and strain
into 3 oz. Cocktail glass.

**CUBAN COCKTAIL
No. 1**

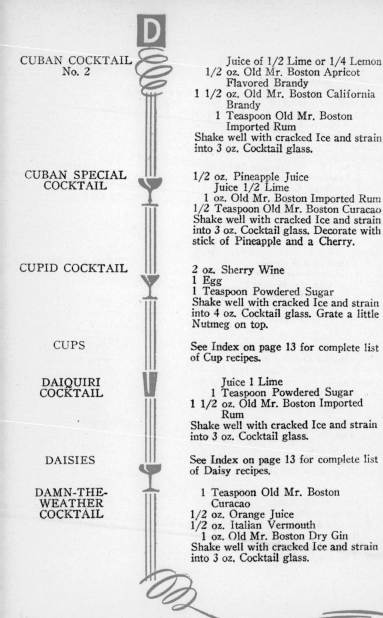

**CUBAN COCKTAIL
No. 2**

Juice of 1/2 Lime or 1/4 Lemon
1/2 oz. Old Mr. Boston Apricot
    Flavored Brandy
1 1/2 oz. Old Mr. Boston California
    Brandy
1 Teaspoon Old Mr. Boston
    Imported Rum
Shake well with cracked Ice and strain
into 3 oz. Cocktail glass.

**CUBAN SPECIAL
COCKTAIL**

1/2 oz. Pineapple Juice
Juice 1/2 Lime
1 oz. Old Mr. Boston Imported Rum
1/2 Teaspoon Old Mr. Boston Curacao
Shake well with cracked Ice and strain
into 3 oz. Cocktail glass. Decorate with
stick of Pineapple and a Cherry.

CUPID COCKTAIL

2 oz. Sherry Wine
1 Egg
1 Teaspoon Powdered Sugar
Shake well with cracked Ice and strain
into 4 oz. Cocktail glass. Grate a little
Nutmeg on top.

CUPS

See Index on page 13 for complete list
of Cup recipes.

**DAIQUIRI
COCKTAIL**

Juice 1 Lime
1 Teaspoon Powdered Sugar
1 1/2 oz. Old Mr. Boston Imported
    Rum
Shake well with cracked Ice and strain
into 3 oz. Cocktail glass.

DAISIES

See Index on page 13 for complete list
of Daisy recipes.

**DAMN-THE-
WEATHER
COCKTAIL**

1 Teaspoon Old Mr. Boston
    Curacao
1/2 oz. Orange Juice
1/2 oz. Italian Vermouth
1 oz. Old Mr. Boston Dry Gin
Shake well with cracked Ice and strain
into 3 oz. Cocktail glass.

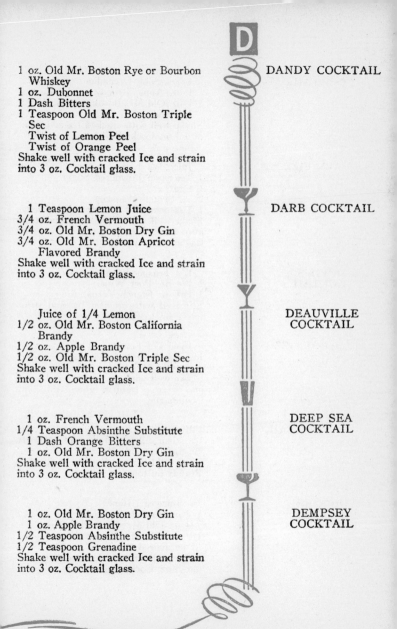

D

DANDY COCKTAIL

1 oz. Old Mr. Boston Rye or Bourbon
    Whiskey
1 oz. Dubonnet
1 Dash Bitters
1 Teaspoon Old Mr. Boston Triple
    Sec
    Twist of Lemon Peel
    Twist of Orange Peel
Shake well with cracked Ice and strain
into 3 oz. Cocktail glass.

DARB COCKTAIL

1 Teaspoon Lemon Juice
3/4 oz. French Vermouth
3/4 oz. Old Mr. Boston Dry Gin
3/4 oz. Old Mr. Boston Apricot
    Flavored Brandy
Shake well with cracked Ice and strain
into 3 oz. Cocktail glass.

DEAUVILLE
COCKTAIL

Juice of 1/4 Lemon
1/2 oz. Old Mr. Boston California
    Brandy
1/2 oz. Apple Brandy
1/2 oz. Old Mr. Boston Triple Sec
Shake well with cracked Ice and strain
into 3 oz. Cocktail glass.

DEEP SEA
COCKTAIL

1 oz. French Vermouth
1/4 Teaspoon Absinthe Substitute
1 Dash Orange Bitters
1 oz. Old Mr. Boston Dry Gin
Shake well with cracked Ice and strain
into 3 oz. Cocktail glass.

DEMPSEY
COCKTAIL

1 oz. Old Mr. Boston Dry Gin
1 oz. Apple Brandy
1/2 Teaspoon Absinthe Substitute
1/2 Teaspoon Grenadine
Shake well with cracked Ice and strain
into 3 oz. Cocktail glass.

D

DEPTH BOMB COCKTAIL

1/4 Teaspoon Lemon Juice
1 Teaspoon Grenadine
1 oz. Apple Brandy
1 oz. Old Mr. Boston California Brandy
Shake well with cracked Ice and strain into 3 oz. Cocktail glass.

DERBY FIZZ

Juice 1/2 Lemon
1 Teaspoon Powdered Sugar
1 Egg
2 oz. Scotch Whiskey
1 Teaspoon Old Mr. Boston Curacao
Shake well with cracked Ice and strain into 8 oz. Highball glass. Fill with Carbonated Water.

DEVIL'S COCKTAIL

1/2 Teaspoon Lemon Juice
1 1/4 oz. Port Wine
1 1/4 oz. French Vermouth
Stir well with cracked Ice and strain into 3 oz. Cocktail glass.

DIAMOND FIZZ

Juice 1/2 Lemon
1 Teaspoon Powdered Sugar
2 oz. Old Mr. Boston Dry Gin
Shake well with cracked Ice and strain into 7 oz. Highball glass. Fill with Champagne.

DIANA COCKTAIL

Fill 3 oz. Cocktail glass with shaved Ice, then fill 3/4 full with Old Mr. Boston Creme de Menthe (White) and float Old Mr. Boston California Brandy on top.

DICK, JR. COCKTAIL

Juice of 1 Lime
1/2 oz. French Vermouth
3/4 oz. Old Mr. Boston Dry Gin
1/2 oz. Old Mr. Boston Apricot Flavored Brandy
Shake well with cracked Ice and strain into 3 oz. Cocktail glass.

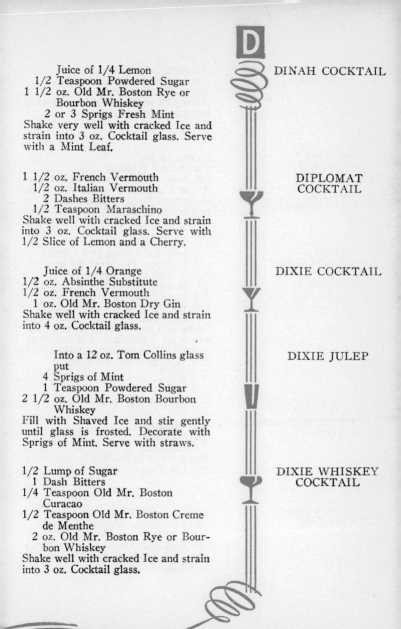

D

DINAH COCKTAIL

Juice of 1/4 Lemon
1/2 Teaspoon Powdered Sugar
1 1/2 oz. Old Mr. Boston Rye or
Bourbon Whiskey
2 or 3 Sprigs Fresh Mint
Shake very well with cracked Ice and
strain into 3 oz. Cocktail glass. Serve
with a Mint Leaf.

DIPLOMAT COCKTAIL

1 1/2 oz. French Vermouth
1/2 oz. Italian Vermouth
2 Dashes Bitters
1/2 Teaspoon Maraschino
Shake well with cracked Ice and strain
into 3 oz. Cocktail glass. Serve with
1/2 Slice of Lemon and a Cherry.

DIXIE COCKTAIL

Juice of 1/4 Orange
1/2 oz. Absinthe Substitute
1/2 oz. French Vermouth
1 oz. Old Mr. Boston Dry Gin
Shake well with cracked Ice and strain
into 4 oz. Cocktail glass.

DIXIE JULEP

Into a 12 oz. Tom Collins glass
put
4 Sprigs of Mint
1 Teaspoon Powdered Sugar
2 1/2 oz. Old Mr. Boston Bourbon
Whiskey
Fill with Shaved Ice and stir gently
until glass is frosted. Decorate with
Sprigs of Mint. Serve with straws.

DIXIE WHISKEY COCKTAIL

1/2 Lump of Sugar
1 Dash Bitters
1/4 Teaspoon Old Mr. Boston
Curacao
1/2 Teaspoon Old Mr. Boston Creme
de Menthe
2 oz. Old Mr. Boston Rye or Bourbon Whiskey
Shake well with cracked Ice and strain
into 3 oz. Cocktail glass.

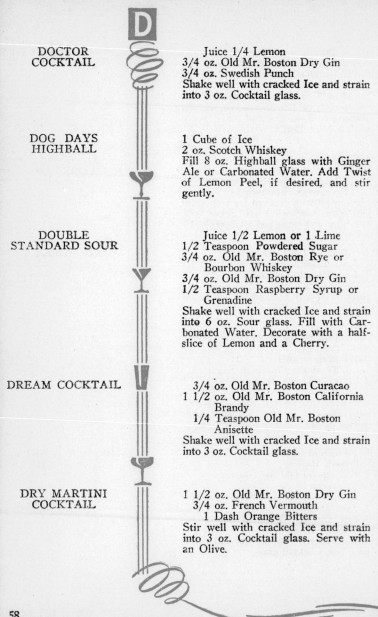

DOCTOR COCKTAIL

Juice 1/4 Lemon
3/4 oz. Old Mr. Boston Dry Gin
3/4 oz. Swedish Punch
Shake well with cracked Ice and strain into 3 oz. Cocktail glass.

DOG DAYS HIGHBALL

1 Cube of Ice
2 oz. Scotch Whiskey
Fill 8 oz. Highball glass with Ginger Ale or Carbonated Water. Add Twist of Lemon Peel, if desired, and stir gently.

DOUBLE STANDARD SOUR

Juice 1/2 Lemon or 1 Lime
1/2 Teaspoon Powdered Sugar
3/4 oz. Old Mr. Boston Rye or Bourbon Whiskey
3/4 oz. Old Mr. Boston Dry Gin
1/2 Teaspoon Raspberry Syrup or Grenadine
Shake well with cracked Ice and strain into 6 oz. Sour glass. Fill with Carbonated Water. Decorate with a half-slice of Lemon and a Cherry.

DREAM COCKTAIL

3/4 oz. Old Mr. Boston Curacao
1 1/2 oz. Old Mr. Boston California Brandy
1/4 Teaspoon Old Mr. Boston Anisette
Shake well with cracked Ice and strain into 3 oz. Cocktail glass.

DRY MARTINI COCKTAIL

1 1/2 oz. Old Mr. Boston Dry Gin
3/4 oz. French Vermouth
1 Dash Orange Bitters
Stir well with cracked Ice and strain into 3 oz. Cocktail glass. Serve with an Olive.

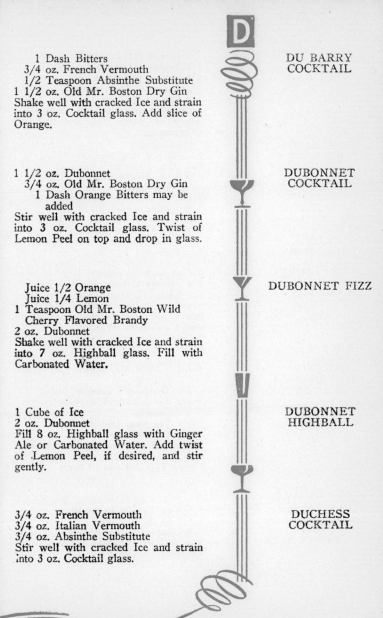

1 Dash Bitters
3/4 oz. French Vermouth
1/2 Teaspoon Absinthe Substitute
1 1/2 oz. Old Mr. Boston Dry Gin
Shake well with cracked Ice and strain into 3 oz. Cocktail glass. Add slice of Orange.

DU BARRY COCKTAIL

1 1/2 oz. Dubonnet
3/4 oz. Old Mr. Boston Dry Gin
1 Dash Orange Bitters may be added
Stir well with cracked Ice and strain into 3 oz. Cocktail glass. Twist of Lemon Peel on top and drop in glass.

DUBONNET COCKTAIL

Juice 1/2 Orange
Juice 1/4 Lemon
1 Teaspoon Old Mr. Boston Wild Cherry Flavored Brandy
2 oz. Dubonnet
Shake well with cracked Ice and strain into 7 oz. Highball glass. Fill with Carbonated Water.

DUBONNET FIZZ

1 Cube of Ice
2 oz. Dubonnet
Fill 8 oz. Highball glass with Ginger Ale or Carbonated Water. Add twist of Lemon Peel, if desired, and stir gently.

DUBONNET HIGHBALL

3/4 oz. French Vermouth
3/4 oz. Italian Vermouth
3/4 oz. Absinthe Substitute
Stir well with cracked Ice and strain into 3 oz. Cocktail glass.

DUCHESS COCKTAIL

59

E

DUKE COCKTAIL

1/2 oz. Old Mr. Boston Triple Sec
1 Teaspoon Orange Juice
2 Teaspoons Lemon Juice
1/2 Teaspoon Maraschino
1 Egg
Shake well with cracked Ice and strain into 8 oz. Stem glass and fill with Champagne.

DUNLOP
COCKTAIL

3/4 oz. Sherry Wine
1 Dash Bitters
1 1/2 oz. Old Mr. Boston Imported Rum
Stir well with cracked Ice and strain into 3 oz. Cocktail glass.

DUTCH MIKE

2 oz. Old Mr. Boston Dry Gin
1/2 Teaspoon Amer Picon
Juice 1/2 Lime
Shake well with cracked Ice and strain into 12 oz. Tom Collins glass and fill with Carbonated Water.

EAST INDIA
COCKTAIL No. 1

1 1/2 oz. Old Mr. Boston California Brandy
1/2 Teaspoon Pineapple Juice
1/2 Teaspoon Old Mr. Boston Curacao
1 Teaspoon Jamaica Rum
1 Dash Bitters
Shake well with cracked Ice and strain into 3 oz. Cocktail glass. Twist of Lemon Peel and add a Cherry.

EAST INDIA
COCKTAIL No. 2

1 1/4 oz. French Vermouth
1 1/4 oz. Sherry Wine
1 Dash Orange Bitters
Stir well with cracked Ice and strain into 3 oz. Cocktail glass.

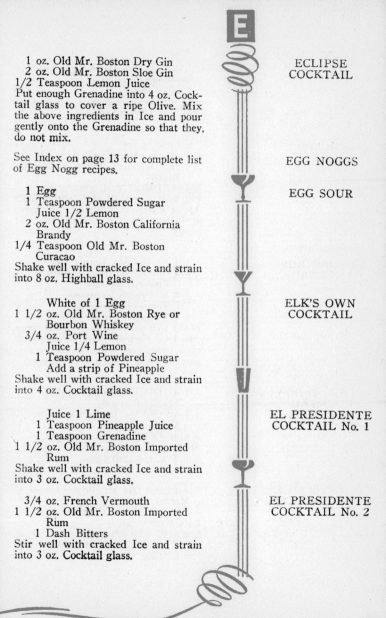

E

1 oz. Old Mr. Boston Dry Gin
2 oz. Old Mr. Boston Sloe Gin
1/2 Teaspoon Lemon Juice
Put enough Grenadine into 4 oz. Cocktail glass to cover a ripe Olive. Mix the above ingredients in Ice and pour gently onto the Grenadine so that they, do not mix.

ECLIPSE
COCKTAIL

See Index on page 13 for complete list of Egg Nogg recipes.

EGG NOGGS

1 Egg
1 Teaspoon Powdered Sugar
Juice 1/2 Lemon
2 oz. Old Mr. Boston California Brandy
1/4 Teaspoon Old Mr. Boston Curacao
Shake well with cracked Ice and strain into 8 oz. Highball glass.

EGG SOUR

White of 1 Egg
1 1/2 oz. Old Mr. Boston Rye or Bourbon Whiskey
3/4 oz. Port Wine
Juice 1/4 Lemon
1 Teaspoon Powdered Sugar
Add a strip of Pineapple
Shake well with cracked Ice and strain into 4 oz. Cocktail glass.

ELK'S OWN
COCKTAIL

Juice 1 Lime
1 Teaspoon Pineapple Juice
1 Teaspoon Grenadine
1 1/2 oz. Old Mr. Boston Imported Rum
Shake well with cracked Ice and strain into 3 oz. Cocktail glass.

EL PRESIDENTE
COCKTAIL No. 1

3/4 oz. French Vermouth
1 1/2 oz. Old Mr. Boston Imported Rum
1 Dash Bitters
Stir well with cracked Ice and strain into 3 oz. Cocktail glass.

EL PRESIDENTE
COCKTAIL No. 2

E

EMERALD ISLE
COCKTAIL

2 oz. Old Mr. Boston Dry Gin
1 Teaspoon Old Mr. Boston Creme
de Menthe (Green)
3 Dashes Bitters
Stir well with cracked Ice and strain
into 3 oz. Cocktail glass.

ENGLISH
HIGHBALL

1 Cube of Ice
3/4 oz. Old Mr. Boston Dry Gin
3/4 oz. Old Mr. Boston California
Brandy
3/4 oz. Italian Vermouth
Fill 8 oz. Highball glass with Ginger
Ale or Carbonated Water. Add Twist
of Lemon Peel, if desired, and stir
gently.

ENGLISH ROSE
COCKTAIL

1 1/4 oz. Old Mr. Boston Dry Gin
3/4 oz. Old Mr. Boston Apricot
Flavored Brandy
3/4 oz. French Vermouth
1 Teaspoon Grenadine
1/4 Teaspoon Lemon Juice
Shake well with cracked Ice and strain
into 4 oz. Cocktail glass. Frost rim of
glass by rubbing with Lemon and dipping in Sugar. Serve with a Cherry.

ETHEL DUFFY
COCKTAIL

3/4 oz. Old Mr. Boston Apricot
Flavored Brandy
3/4 oz. Old Mr. Boston Creme de
Menthe (White)
3/4 oz. Old Mr. Boston Curacao
Shake well with cracked Ice and strain
into 3 oz. Cocktail glass.

EVERYBODY'S
IRISH COCKTAIL

1 Teaspoon Old Mr. Boston Creme de
Menthe (Green)
1 Teaspoon Green Chartreuse
2 oz. Irish Whiskey
Stir well with cracked Ice and strain
into 3 oz. Cocktail glass. Serve with
Green Olive.

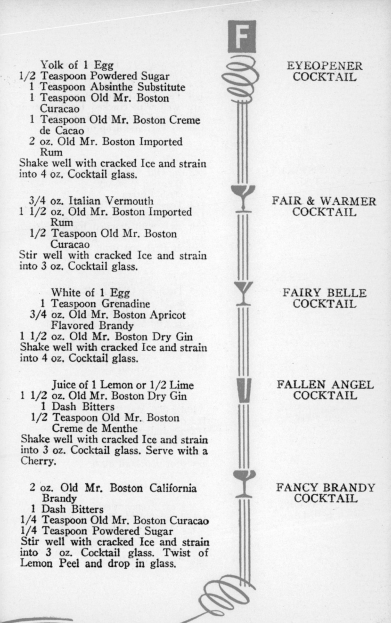

Yolk of 1 Egg
1/2 Teaspoon Powdered Sugar
1 Teaspoon Absinthe Substitute
1 Teaspoon Old Mr. Boston
   Curacao
1 Teaspoon Old Mr. Boston Creme
   de Cacao
2 oz. Old Mr. Boston Imported
   Rum
Shake well with cracked Ice and strain
into 4 oz. Cocktail glass.

EYEOPENER COCKTAIL

3/4 oz. Italian Vermouth
1 1/2 oz. Old Mr. Boston Imported
   Rum
1/2 Teaspoon Old Mr. Boston
   Curacao
Stir well with cracked Ice and strain
into 3 oz. Cocktail glass.

FAIR & WARMER COCKTAIL

White of 1 Egg
1 Teaspoon Grenadine
3/4 oz. Old Mr. Boston Apricot
   Flavored Brandy
1 1/2 oz. Old Mr. Boston Dry Gin
Shake well with cracked Ice and strain
into 4 oz. Cocktail glass.

FAIRY BELLE COCKTAIL

Juice of 1 Lemon or 1/2 Lime
1 1/2 oz. Old Mr. Boston Dry Gin
1 Dash Bitters
1/2 Teaspoon Old Mr. Boston
   Creme de Menthe
Shake well with cracked Ice and strain
into 3 oz. Cocktail glass. Serve with a
Cherry.

FALLEN ANGEL COCKTAIL

2 oz. Old Mr. Boston California
   Brandy
1 Dash Bitters
1/4 Teaspoon Old Mr. Boston Curacao
1/4 Teaspoon Powdered Sugar
Stir well with cracked Ice and strain
into 3 oz. Cocktail glass. Twist of
Lemon Peel and drop in glass.

FANCY BRANDY COCKTAIL

F

FANCY GIN COCKTAIL

2 oz. Old Mr. Boston Dry Gin
1 Dash Bitters
1/4 Teaspoon Old Mr. Boston Curacao
1/4 Teaspoon Powdered Sugar
Stir well with cracked Ice and strain into 3 oz. Cocktail glass. Twist of Lemon Peel and drop in glass.

FANCY WHISKEY COCKTAIL

2 oz. Old Mr. Boston Rye or Bourbon Whiskey
1 Dash Bitters
1/4 Teaspoon Old Mr. Boston Curacao
1/4 Teaspoon Powdered Sugar
Stir well with cracked Ice and strain into 3 oz. Cocktail glass. Twist of Lemon Peel and drop in glass.

FANTASIO COCKTAIL

1 Teaspoon Old Mr. Boston Creme de Menthe (White)
1 Teaspoon Maraschino
1 oz. Old Mr. Boston California Brandy
3/4 oz. French Vermouth
Stir well with cracked Ice and strain into 3 oz. Cocktail glass.

FARMER'S COCKTAIL

1 oz. Old Mr. Boston Dry Gin
1/2 oz. French Vermouth
1/2 oz. Italian Vermouth
2 Dashes Bitters
Shake well with cracked Ice and strain into 3 oz. Cocktail glass.

FASCINATOR COCKTAIL

3/4 oz. French Vermouth
1 1/2 oz. Old Mr. Boston Dry Gin
1/2 Teaspoon Absinthe Substitute
1 Sprig Fresh Mint
Shake well with cracked Ice and strain into 3 oz. Cocktail glass.

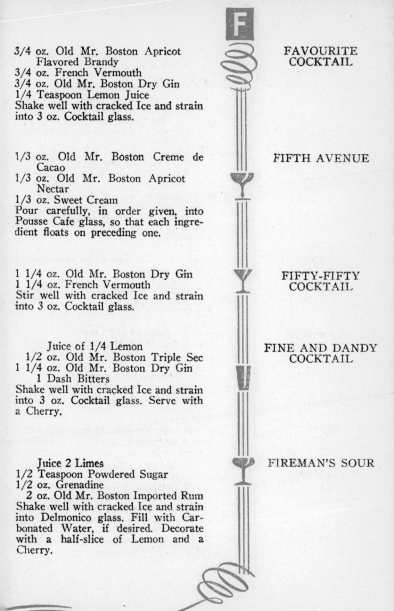

3/4 oz. Old Mr. Boston Apricot
    Flavored Brandy
3/4 oz. French Vermouth
3/4 oz. Old Mr. Boston Dry Gin
1/4 Teaspoon Lemon Juice
Shake well with cracked Ice and strain
into 3 oz. Cocktail glass.

FAVOURITE COCKTAIL

1/3 oz. Old Mr. Boston Creme de
    Cacao
1/3 oz. Old Mr. Boston Apricot
    Nectar
1/3 oz. Sweet Cream
Pour carefully, in order given, into
Pousse Cafe glass, so that each ingredient floats on preceding one.

FIFTH AVENUE

1 1/4 oz. Old Mr. Boston Dry Gin
1 1/4 oz. French Vermouth
Stir well with cracked Ice and strain
into 3 oz. Cocktail glass.

FIFTY-FIFTY COCKTAIL

Juice of 1/4 Lemon
1/2 oz. Old Mr. Boston Triple Sec
1 1/4 oz. Old Mr. Boston Dry Gin
1 Dash Bitters
Shake well with cracked Ice and strain
into 3 oz. Cocktail glass. Serve with
a Cherry.

FINE AND DANDY COCKTAIL

Juice 2 Limes
1/2 Teaspoon Powdered Sugar
1/2 oz. Grenadine
2 oz. Old Mr. Boston Imported Rum
Shake well with cracked Ice and strain
into Delmonico glass. Fill with Carbonated Water, if desired. Decorate
with a half-slice of Lemon and a
Cherry.

FIREMAN'S SOUR

F

FISH HOUSE PUNCH

Juice of 1 Dozen Lemons
Add enough Powdered Sugar to sweeten
1 qt. Carbonated Water
Place large block of Ice in Punch bowl and stir well.
Then add:
1 1/2 qts. Old Mr. Boston California Brandy
1 pt. Old Mr. Boston Peach Flavored Brandy
1 pt. Old Mr. Boston Imported Rum

Some prefer to add the strained contents of a Pot of Tea. Stir well and decorate with fruits in season. Serve in 4 oz. Punch glasses.

FIXES

See Index on page 13 for complete list of Fix recipes.

FIZZES

See Index on page 13 for complete list of Fizz recipes.

FLAMINGO COCKTAIL

Juice of 1/2 Lime
1/2 oz. Old Mr. Boston Apricot Nectar Liqueur
1 1/4 oz. Old Mr. Boston Dry Gin
1 Teaspoon Grenadine

Shake well with cracked Ice and strain into 3 oz. Cocktail glass.

FLIPS

See Index on page 14 for complete list of Flip recipes.

FLORADORA COOLER

Into 12 oz. Tom Collins glass, put:
Juice 1 Lime
1/2 Teaspoon Powdered Sugar
1/2 oz. Raspberry Syrup or Grenadine
2 oz. Carbonated Water, and stir.
Fill glass with cracked Ice and add:
2 oz. Old Mr. Boston Dry Gin.
Fill with Carbonated Water or Ginger Ale.

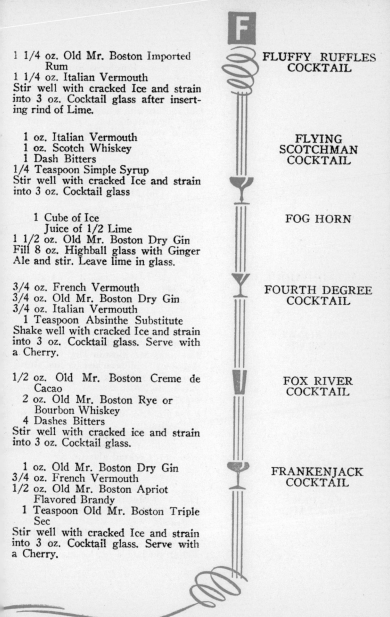

F

1 1/4 oz. Old Mr. Boston Imported
    Rum
1 1/4 oz. Italian Vermouth
Stir well with cracked Ice and strain
into 3 oz. Cocktail glass after insert-
ing rind of Lime.

FLUFFY RUFFLES
COCKTAIL

1 oz. Italian Vermouth
1 oz. Scotch Whiskey
1 Dash Bitters
1/4 Teaspoon Simple Syrup
Stir well with cracked Ice and strain
into 3 oz. Cocktail glass

FLYING
SCOTCHMAN
COCKTAIL

1 Cube of Ice
   Juice of 1/2 Lime
1 1/2 oz. Old Mr. Boston Dry Gin
Fill 8 oz. Highball glass with Ginger
Ale and stir. Leave lime in glass.

FOG HORN

3/4 oz. French Vermouth
3/4 oz. Old Mr. Boston Dry Gin
3/4 oz. Italian Vermouth
  1 Teaspoon Absinthe Substitute
Shake well with cracked Ice and strain
into 3 oz. Cocktail glass. Serve with
a Cherry.

FOURTH DEGREE
COCKTAIL

1/2 oz. Old Mr. Boston Creme de
    Cacao
  2 oz. Old Mr. Boston Rye or
    Bourbon Whiskey
  4 Dashes Bitters
Stir well with cracked ice and strain
into 3 oz. Cocktail glass.

FOX RIVER
COCKTAIL

1 oz. Old Mr. Boston Dry Gin
3/4 oz. French Vermouth
1/2 oz. Old Mr. Boston Apriot
    Flavored Brandy
  1 Teaspoon Old Mr. Boston Triple
    Sec
Stir well with cracked Ice and strain
into 3 oz. Cocktail glass. Serve with
a Cherry.

FRANKENJACK
COCKTAIL

FRENCH "75"

Juice of 1 Lemon
2 Teaspoons Powdered Sugar
1 Cube of Ice
Stir well in 12 oz. Tom Collins glass.
Then add 2 oz. Old Mr. Boston Dry
Gin and fill with Champagne. Decorate
with slice of Lemon, Orange and a
Cherry. Serve with straws.

FRISCO SOUR

Juice 1/4 Lemon
Juice 1/2 Lime
1/2 oz. Raspberry Syrup or Grenadine
2 oz. Old Mr. Boston Rye or Bourbon Whiskey
Shake well with cracked Ice and strain
into 6 oz. Sour glass. Fill with Carbonated Water.

**FROSTED DAIQUIRI
COCKTAIL**

See West Indies Frosted Cocktail on
Page 149.

**FROTH BLOWER
COCKTAIL**

White of 1 Egg
1 Teaspoon Grenadine
2 oz. Old Mr. Boston Dry Gin
Shake well with cracked Ice and strain
into 4 oz. Cocktail glass.

**FROUPE
COCKTAIL**

1 1/4 oz. Italian Vermouth
1 1/4 oz. Old Mr. Boston California
Brandy
1 Teaspoon Benedictine
Stir well with cracked Ice and strain
into 3 oz. Cocktail glass.

**GASPER
COCKTAIL**

1 oz. Old Mr. Boston Dry Gin
1 oz. Old Mr. Boston Apricot Flavored
Brandy
If desired add a very little Powdered
Sugar. Shake well with cracked Ice
and strain into 3 oz. Cocktail glass.

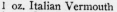

G

1 oz. Italian Vermouth
1 oz. Old Mr. Boston California
   Brandy
1 Teaspoon Powdered Sugar
1 Teaspoon Lemon Juice
Shake well with cracked Ice and strain
into 3 oz. Cocktail glass.

GAZETTE
COCKTAIL

1 Egg
1 Teaspoon Powdered Sugar
Shake well with cracked Ice and strain
into 12 oz. Tom Collins glass. Fill
glass with Claret or Sweet Cider.
Grate Nutmeg on top.

GENERAL
HARRISON'S
EGG NOGG

1 1/2 oz. Old Mr. Boston Dry Gin
  1/2 oz. French Vermouth
Shake well with cracked Ice and strain
into 3 oz. Cocktail Glass. Twist of
Lemon Peel and serve with 3 Pearl
Onions.

GIBSON
COCKTAIL

   Juice of 1/4 Lemon
1/2 oz. French Vermouth
3/4 oz. Old Mr. Boston Wild Cherry
   Flavored Brandy
3/4 oz. Old Mr. Boston Dry Gin
  1 Dash Orange Bitters
Stir well with cracked Ice and strain
into 3 oz. Cocktail glass.

GILROY
COCKTAIL

   Juice 1 Lime
  1 Teaspoon Powdered Sugar
1 1/2 oz. Old Mr. Boston Dry Gin
Shake well with cracked Ice and strain
into 4 oz. Cocktail glass and fill balance with Carbonated Water.

GIMLET
COCKTAIL

Put 1/2 Teaspoon Bitters into 3 oz.
Cocktail glass and revolve glass until
it is entirely coated with the Bitters.
Then fill with Old Mr. Boston Dry
Gin. No Ice is used in this drink.

GIN AND BITTERS

G

GIN AND IT
(English)

2 oz. Old Mr. Boston Dry Gin
1 oz. Italian Vermouth
Stir. No Ice is used in this drink.

GIN and TONIC

2 oz. Old Mr. Boston Dry Gin
  Juice 1/2 Lime—Drop Peel in glass
  Cube of Ice
Fill glass with Quinine Water and
stir. Use 12 oz. Tom Collins glass.

GIN BUCK

1 Cube of Ice
  Juice of 1/2 Lemon
1 1/2 oz. Old Mr. Boston Dry Gin
Fill 8 oz. Highball glass with Ginger
Ale and stir.

GIN COBBLER

1 Teaspoon Powdered Sugar
2 oz. Carbonated Water
  Fill 8 oz. Goblet with Shaved Ice
  Add 2 oz. Old Mr. Boston Dry Gin
Stir well and decorate with fruits in
season. Serve with straws.

GIN COCKTAIL

2 oz. Old Mr. Boston Dry Gin
2 Dashes Bitters
Stir well with cracked Ice and strain
into 3 oz. Cocktail glass. Serve with
a Twist of Lemon Peel and drop in
glass.

GIN COOLER

  Into 12 oz. Tom Collins glass, put:
1/2 Teaspoon Powdered Sugar
  2 oz. Carbonated Water, and stir
    Fill glass with cracked Ice and
    add:
  2 oz. Old Mr. Boston Dry Gin
    Fill with Carbonated Water or
    Ginger Ale
Insert spiral of Orange or Lemon Peel
(or both) and dangle end over rim
of glass.

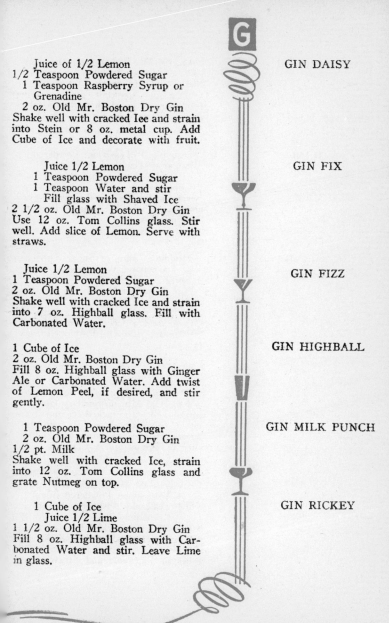

G

Juice of 1/2 Lemon
1/2 Teaspoon Powdered Sugar
1 Teaspoon Raspberry Syrup or
   Grenadine
2 oz. Old Mr. Boston Dry Gin
Shake well with cracked Ice and strain
into Stein or 8 oz. metal cup. Add
Cube of Ice and decorate with fruit.

GIN DAISY

Juice 1/2 Lemon
1 Teaspoon Powdered Sugar
1 Teaspoon Water and stir
   Fill glass with Shaved Ice
2 1/2 oz. Old Mr. Boston Dry Gin
Use 12 oz. Tom Collins glass. Stir
well. Add slice of Lemon. Serve with
straws.

GIN FIX

Juice 1/2 Lemon
1 Teaspoon Powdered Sugar
2 oz. Old Mr. Boston Dry Gin
Shake well with cracked Ice and strain
into 7 oz. Highball glass. Fill with
Carbonated Water.

GIN FIZZ

1 Cube of Ice
2 oz. Old Mr. Boston Dry Gin
Fill 8 oz. Highball glass with Ginger
Ale or Carbonated Water. Add twist
of Lemon Peel, if desired, and stir
gently.

GIN HIGHBALL

1 Teaspoon Powdered Sugar
2 oz. Old Mr. Boston Dry Gin
1/2 pt. Milk
Shake well with cracked Ice, strain
into 12 oz. Tom Collins glass and
grate Nutmeg on top.

GIN MILK PUNCH

1 Cube of Ice
Juice 1/2 Lime
1 1/2 oz. Old Mr. Boston Dry Gin
Fill 8 oz. Highball glass with Carbonated Water and stir. Leave Lime
in glass.

GIN RICKEY

G

GIN SANGAREE

1 1/2 oz. Old Mr. Boston Dry Gin
1 Teaspoon Powdered Sugar
Shake well with cracked Ice and strain into 3 oz. Cocktail glass, leaving enough room in which to float a tablespoon of Port Wine.

GIN SLING

Dissolve 1 Teaspoon Powdered Sugar in Teaspoon of Water.
2 oz. Old Mr. Boston Dry Gin
2 Cubes of Ice
Serve in Old Fashioned Cocktail glass and stir. Twist of Orange Peel and drop in glass.

GIN SMASH

Muddle 1 Lump of Sugar with
1 oz. Carbonated Water and
4 Sprigs of Green Mint
Add 2 oz. Old Mr. Boston Dry Gin, then a Cube of Ice.
Stir and decorate with a slice of Orange and a Cherry. Twist Lemon Peel on top. Use Old Fashioned Cocktail glass.

GIN SOUR

Juice 1/2 Lemon
1/2 Teaspoon Powdered Sugar
2 oz. Old Mr. Boston Dry Gin
Shake well with cracked Ice and strain into 6 oz. Sour glass. Fill with Carbonated Water. Decorate with a half-slice of Lemon and a Cherry.

GIN SQUIRT

1 1/2 oz. Old Mr. Boston Dry Gin
1 Tablespoon Powdered Sugar
1 Teaspoon Raspberry Syrup or Grenadine
Stir well with cracked Ice and strain into 8 oz. Highball glass and fill with Carbonated Water. Decorate with cubes of Pineapple and Strawberries.

G

GIN SWIZZLE

Into 12 oz. Tom Collins glass, put:
Juice 1 Lime
1 Teaspoon Powdered Sugar
2 oz. Carbonated Water
Fill glass with shaved Ice and stir thoroughly with swizzle stick. Then add:
2 Dashes Bitters
2 oz. Old Mr. Boston Dry Gin
Fill with Carbonated Water and serve with swizzle stick in glass, allowing individual to do final stirring.

GIN TODDY

Use Old Fashioned Cocktail glass.
1/2 Teaspoon Powdered Sugar
2 Teaspoons Water
2 oz. Old Mr. Boston Dry Gin
1 Lump of Ice
Stir well and Twist Lemon Peel on top.

GIN TODDY
(Hot)

Put Lump of Sugar into Hot Whiskey glass and fill with two-third Boiling Water. Add 2 oz. Old Mr. Boston Dry Gin. Stir and decorate with slice of Lemon. Grate Nutmeg on top.

GOLDEN FIZZ

Juice of 1/2 Lemon
1 Teaspoon Powdered Sugar
2 oz. Old Mr. Boston Dry Gin
Yolk of 1 Egg
Shake well with cracked Ice and strain into 8 oz. Highball glass. Fill with Carbonated Water.

GOLDEN GATE
COCKTAIL

1 1/2 oz. Old Mr. Boston Dry Gin
1 Scoop Orange Sherbet
Shake well and strain into 4 oz. Cocktail glass.

GOLDEN MARTINI COCKTAIL

1 1/2 oz. Old Mr. Boston Orange Flavored Gin
3/4 oz. French Vermouth
1 Dash Bitters
Stir well with cracked Ice and strain into 3 oz. Cocktail glass. Serve with an Olive.

GOLDEN SLIPPER COCKTAIL

3/4 oz. Yellow Chartreuse
2 oz. Old Mr. Boston Apricot Nectar Liqueur
Shake well with cracked Ice and strain into 4 oz. Cocktail glass. Float Yolk of Egg on top.

GOLF COCKTAIL

1 1/2 oz. Old Mr. Boston Dry Gin
3/4 oz. French Vermouth
2 Dashes Bitters
Stir well with cracked Ice and strain into 3 oz. Cocktail glass.

GRAND ROYAL FIZZ

Juice 1/4 Orange
Juice 1/2 Lemon
1 Teaspoon Powdered Sugar
2 oz. Old Mr. Boston Dry Gin
1/2 Teaspoon Maraschino
2 Teaspoons Sweet Cream
Shake well with cracked Ice and strain into 8 oz. Highball glass. Fill with Carbonated Water.

GRAPEFRUIT COCKTAIL

1 oz. Grapefruit Juice
1 oz. Old Mr. Boston Dry Gin
1 Teaspoon Maraschino
Shake well with cracked Ice and strain into 3 oz. Cocktail glass. Serve with a Cherry.

GRAPE VINE COCKTAIL

Juice 1/4 Lemon
1/2 oz. Grape Juice
1 1/4 oz. Old Mr. Boston Dry Gin
1/4 Teaspoon Grenadine
Stir well with cracked Ice and strain into 3 oz. Cocktail glass.

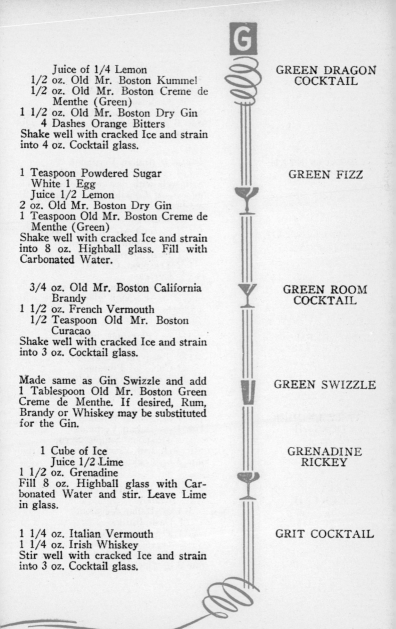

G

Juice of 1/4 Lemon
1/2 oz. Old Mr. Boston Kummel
1/2 oz. Old Mr. Boston Creme de Menthe (Green)
1 1/2 oz. Old Mr. Boston Dry Gin
4 Dashes Orange Bitters
Shake well with cracked Ice and strain into 4 oz. Cocktail glass.

GREEN DRAGON COCKTAIL

1 Teaspoon Powdered Sugar
White 1 Egg
Juice 1/2 Lemon
2 oz. Old Mr. Boston Dry Gin
1 Teaspoon Old Mr. Boston Creme de Menthe (Green)
Shake well with cracked Ice and strain into 8 oz. Highball glass. Fill with Carbonated Water.

GREEN FIZZ

3/4 oz. Old Mr. Boston California Brandy
1 1/2 oz. French Vermouth
1/2 Teaspoon Old Mr. Boston Curacao
Shake well with cracked Ice and strain into 3 oz. Cocktail glass.

GREEN ROOM COCKTAIL

Made same as Gin Swizzle and add 1 Tablespoon Old Mr. Boston Green Creme de Menthe. If desired, Rum, Brandy or Whiskey may be substituted for the Gin.

GREEN SWIZZLE

1 Cube of Ice
Juice 1/2 Lime
1 1/2 oz. Grenadine
Fill 8 oz. Highball glass with Carbonated Water and stir. Leave Lime in glass.

GRENADINE RICKEY

1 1/4 oz. Italian Vermouth
1 1/4 oz. Irish Whiskey
Stir well with cracked Ice and strain into 3 oz. Cocktail glass.

GRIT COCKTAIL

H

GUARD'S
COCKTAIL

3/4 oz. Italian Vermouth
1 1/2 oz. Mr. Boston Dry Gin
1/2 Teaspoon Old Mr. Boston
Curacao
Stir well with cracked Ice and strain
into 3 oz. Cocktail glass. Serve with
a Cherry.

GYPSY COCKTAIL

1 1/4 oz. Italian Vermouth
1 1/4 oz. Old Mr. Boston Dry Gin
Stir well with cracked Ice and strain
into 3 oz. Cocktail glass. Serve with
a Cherry.

HAKAM COCKTAIL

1 1/4 oz. Old Mr. Boston Dry Gin
1 1/4 oz. Italian Vermouth
1 Dash Orange Bitters
1/2 Teaspoon Old Mr. Boston
Curacao
Stir well with cracked Ice and strain
into 3 oz. Cocktail glass. Serve with
a Cherry.

HARLEM
COCKTAIL

3/4 oz. Pineapple Juice
1 1/2 oz. Old Mr. Boston Dry Gin
1/2 Teaspoon Maraschino
2 Cubes of Pineapple
Shake well with cracked Ice and strain
into 3 oz. Cocktail glass.

HARRY LAUDER
COCKTAIL

1 1/4 oz. Scotch Whiskey
1 1/4 oz. Italian Vermouth
1/2 Teaspoon Simple Syrup
Stir well with cracked Ice and strain
into 3 oz. Cocktail glass.

HARVARD
COCKTAIL

1 1/2 oz. Old Mr. Boston California
Brandy
3/4 oz. Italian Vermouth
1 Dash Bitters
1 Teaspoon Grenadine
2 Teaspoons Lemon Juice
Stir well with cracked Ice and strain
into 3 oz. Cocktail glass.

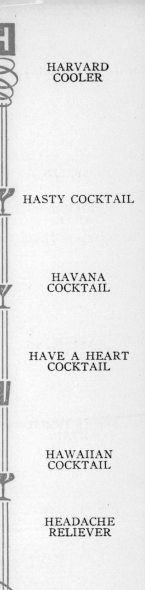

HARVARD COOLER

Into 12 oz. Tom Collins glass, put:
1/2 Teaspoon Powdered Sugar
  2 oz. Carbonated Water, and stir.
    Fill glass with cracked Ice and add:
  2 oz. Applejack
    Fill with Carbonated Water or Ginger Ale
Insert spiral of Orange or Lemon Peel (or both) and dangle end over rim of glass.

HASTY COCKTAIL

  3/4 oz. French Vermouth
1 1/2 oz. Old Mr. Boston Dry Gin
  1/4 Teaspoon Absinthe Substitute
   1 Teaspoon Grenadine
Stir well with cracked Ice and strain into 3 oz. Cocktail glass.

HAVANA COCKTAIL

1 1/4 oz. Pineapple Juice
  3/4 oz. Old Mr. Boston Imported Rum
  1/2 Teaspoon Lemon Juice
Shake well with cracked Ice and strain into 3 oz. Cocktail glass.

HAVE A HEART COCKTAIL

  3/4 oz. Swedish Punch
1 1/2 oz. Old Mr. Boston Dry Gin
  1/2 Teaspoon Grenadine
    Juice of 1/2 Lime
Shake well with cracked Ice and strain into 4 oz. Cocktail glass. Serve with Pineapple on edge with Cherry on Pineapple.

HAWAIIAN COCKTAIL

2 oz. Old Mr. Boston Dry Gin
1/2 oz. Pineapple Juice
1/2 oz. Old Mr. Boston Curacao
Shake well with cracked Ice and strain into 4 oz. Cocktail glass.

HEADACHE RELIEVER

Take two Tom Collins glasses. Put a teaspoonful of Bromo Seltzer into one and fill the other half full of water. Pour from one glass to the other until thoroughly mixed and drink at once.

77

HI-DE-HO SPECIAL

2 oz. Old Mr. Boston Orange
   Flavored Gin
   Juice of 1/2 Lemon
1 Teaspoon Powdered Sugar
Add cracked Ice, stir and strain into
8 oz. Highball glass. Then fill with
Seltzer Water. Decorate with slice of
Lemon.

HIGHBALLS

See Index on page 14 for complete list
of Highball recipes.

**HIGHLAND
COOLER**

   Into 12 oz. Tom Collins glass, put:
1/2 Teaspoon Powdered Sugar
   2 oz. Carbonated Water, and stir.
      Fill glass with cracked Ice and
      add:
   2 oz. Scotch Whiskey.
      Fill with Carbonated Water or
      Ginger Ale
Insert spiral of Orange or Lemon Peel
(or both) and dangle end over rim of
glass.

**HIGHLAND FLING
COCKTAIL**

   3/4 oz. Italian Vermouth
1 1/2 oz. Scotch Whiskey
   2 Dashes Orange Bitters
Shake well with cracked Ice and strain
into 3 oz. Cocktail glass. Serve with
an Olive.

**HOFFMAN HOUSE
COCKTAIL**

   3/4 oz. French Vermouth
1 1/2 oz. Old Mr. Boston Dry Gin
   2 Dashes Orange Bitters
Stir well with cracked Ice and strain
into 3 oz. Cocktail glass. Serve with
an Olive.

**HOLE-IN-ONE
COCKTAIL**

1 1/2 oz. Scotch Whiskey
   3/4 oz. French Vermouth
   1/4 Teaspoon Lemon Juice
   1 Dash Orange Bitters
Shake well with cracked Ice and strain
into 3 oz. Cocktail glass.

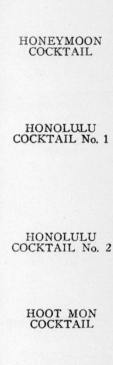

1 Slice of Orange
1 1/2 oz. Old Mr. Boston Dry Gin
3/4 oz. Italian Vermouth
Shake well with cracked Ice and strain into 3 oz. Cocktail glass.

HOMESTEAD COCKTAIL

3/4 oz. Benedictine
3/4 oz. Apple Brandy
Juice of 1/2 Lemon
1 Teaspoon Old Mr. Boston Curacao
Shake well with cracked Ice and strain into 3 oz. Cocktail glass.

HONEYMOON COCKTAIL

1 Dash Bitters
1/4 Teaspoon Orange Juice
1/4 Teaspoon Pineapple Juice
1/4 Teaspoon Lemon Juice
1/2 Teaspoon Powdered Sugar
1 1/2 oz. Old Mr. Boston Dry Gin
Shake well with cracked Ice and strain into 3 oz. Cocktail glass.

HONOLULU COCKTAIL No. 1

3/4 oz. Old Mr. Boston Dry Gin
3/4 oz. Maraschino
3/4 oz. Benedictine
Stir well with cracked Ice and strain into 3 oz. Cocktail glass.

HONOLULU COCKTAIL No. 2

3/4 oz. Italian Vermouth
1 1/2 oz. Scotch Whiskey
1 Teaspoon Benedictine
Stir well with cracked Ice and strain into 3 oz. Cocktail glass. Twist of Lemon Peel and drop in glass.

HOOT MON COCKTAIL

Juice 1/2 Lime
3/4 oz. Old Mr. Boston Apricot Flavored Brandy
3/4 oz. Old Mr. Boston Imported Rum
Stir well with cracked Ice and strain into 3 oz. Cocktail glass.

HOP TOAD COCKTAIL

H

HORSES NECK
(With a Kick)

Peel rind of whole Lemon in spiral fashion and put in 12 oz. Tom Collins glass with one end hanging over the rim. Fill glass with ice cubes. Add 2 oz. Old Mr. Boston Rye or Bourbon Whiskey. Then fill with Ginger Ale and stir well.

HOT BRANDY
FLIP

1 Egg
1 Teaspoon Powdered Sugar
1 1/2 oz. Old Mr. Boston California Brandy
Beat Egg, Sugar and Brandy and pour into hot Tom & Jerry Mug and fill with hot Milk. Grate Nutmeg on top.

HOT BRICK
TODDY

Into Hot Whiskey glass, put:
1 Teaspoon Butter
1 Teaspoon Powdered Sugar
3 Pinches Cinnamon
1 oz. Hot Water, and dissolve thoroughly. Then add:
1 1/2 oz. Old Mr. Boston Rye or Bourbon Whiskey
Fill with boiling Water and stir.

HOT BUTTERED
RUM

Put Lump of Sugar into Hot Whiskey glass and fill with two-thirds Boiling Water. Add square of Butter and 2 oz. Old Mr. Boston Imported Rum. Stir and grate Nutmeg on top.

HOT SPRINGS
COCKTAIL

1 1/2 oz. Dry White Wine
1/2 oz. Pineapple Juice
1/2 Teaspoon Maraschino
1 Dash Orange Bitters
Shake well with cracked Ice and strain into 3 oz. Cocktail glass.

HOT TODDIES

See Index on page 15 for complete list of Toddy recipes.

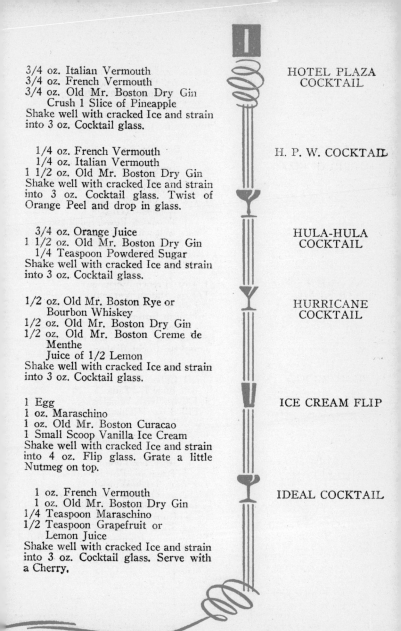

3/4 oz. Italian Vermouth
3/4 oz. French Vermouth
3/4 oz. Old Mr. Boston Dry Gin
    Crush 1 Slice of Pineapple
Shake well with cracked Ice and strain
into 3 oz. Cocktail glass.

HOTEL PLAZA COCKTAIL

1/4 oz. French Vermouth
1/4 oz. Italian Vermouth
1 1/2 oz. Old Mr. Boston Dry Gin
Shake well with cracked Ice and strain
into 3 oz. Cocktail glass. Twist of
Orange Peel and drop in glass.

H. P. W. COCKTAIL

3/4 oz. Orange Juice
1 1/2 oz. Old Mr. Boston Dry Gin
1/4 Teaspoon Powdered Sugar
Shake well with cracked Ice and strain
into 3 oz. Cocktail glass.

HULA-HULA COCKTAIL

1/2 oz. Old Mr. Boston Rye or
    Bourbon Whiskey
1/2 oz. Old Mr. Boston Dry Gin
1/2 oz. Old Mr. Boston Creme de
    Menthe
    Juice of 1/2 Lemon
Shake well with cracked Ice and strain
into 3 oz. Cocktail glass.

HURRICANE COCKTAIL

1 Egg
1 oz. Maraschino
1 oz. Old Mr. Boston Curacao
1 Small Scoop Vanilla Ice Cream
Shake well with cracked Ice and strain
into 4 oz. Flip glass. Grate a little
Nutmeg on top.

ICE CREAM FLIP

1 oz. French Vermouth
1 oz. Old Mr. Boston Dry Gin
1/4 Teaspoon Maraschino
1/2 Teaspoon Grapefruit or
    Lemon Juice
Shake well with cracked Ice and strain
into 3 oz. Cocktail glass. Serve with
a Cherry.

IDEAL COCKTAIL

IMPERIAL COCKTAIL

1 1/4 oz. French Vermouth
1 1/4 oz. Old Mr. Boston Dry Gin
1/4 Teaspoon Maraschino
1 Dash Bitters
Stir well with cracked Ice and strain into 3 oz. Cocktail glass. Serve with a Cherry.

IMPERIAL FIZZ

Juice 1/2 Lemon
1/2 oz. Old Mr. Boston Imported Rum
1 1/2 oz. Old Mr. Boston Rye or Bourbon Whiskey
1 Teaspoon Powdered Sugar
Shake well with cracked Ice and strain into 7 oz. Highball glass. Fill with Carbonated Water.

INCOME TAX COCKTAIL

1/4 oz. French Vermouth
1/4 oz. Italian Vermouth
1 oz. Old Mr. Boston Dry Gin
1 Dash Bitters
Juice of 1/4 Orange
Shake well with cracked Ice and strain into 3 oz. Cocktail glass.

IRISH RICKEY

1 Cube of Ice
Juice 1/2 Lime
1 1/2 oz. Irish Whiskey
Fill 8 oz. Highball glass with Carbonated Water and stir. Leave Lime in glass.

IRISH SHILLELAH

Juice 1/2 Lemon
1 Teaspoon Powdered Sugar
1 1/2 oz. Irish Whiskey
1/2 oz. Old Mr. Boston Sloe Gin
1/2 oz. Old Mr. Boston Imported Rum
2 Slices of Peach
Shake well with cracked Ice and strain into 5 oz. Punch glass. Decorate with Fresh Raspberries, Strawberries and a Cherry.

1/2 Teaspoon Old Mr. Boston
   Curacao
1/2 Teaspoon Absinthe Substitute
1/4 Teaspoon Maraschino
  1 Dash Bitters
  2 oz. Irish Whiskey
Stir well with cracked Ice and strain
into 3 oz. Cocktail glass. Serve with
an Olive.

IRISH WHISKEY COCKTAIL

1 Cube of Ice
2 oz. Irish Whiskey
Fill 8 oz. Highball glass with Ginger
Ale or Carbonated Water. Add twist
of Lemon Peel, if desired, and stir
gently.

IRISH WHISKEY HIGHBALL

1 oz. Applejack
1 oz. Pineapple Juice
  Dash of Bitters
Shake well with cracked Ice and strain
into 3 oz. Cocktail glass.

JACK-IN-THE-BOX COCKTAIL

3/4 oz. Old Mr. Boston Dry Gin
3/4 oz. French Vermouth
1/4 oz. Old Mr. Boston Apricot
   Nectar Liqueur
1/4 oz. Old Mr. Boston Triple Sec
Shake well with cracked Ice and strain
into 3 oz. Cocktail glass.

JACK RABBIT COCKTAIL

1 1/2 oz. Applejack
  Juice 1/2 Lime
  1 Teaspoon Grenadine
Shake well with cracked Ice and strain
into 3 oz. Cocktail glass.

JACK ROSE COCKTAIL

1 oz. Old Mr. Boston Dry Gin
1/2 oz. Claret
1/2 oz. Orange Juice
  1 Teaspoon Jamaica Rum
Shake well with cracked Ice and strain
into 3 oz. Cocktail glass.

JAMAICA GLOW COCKTAIL

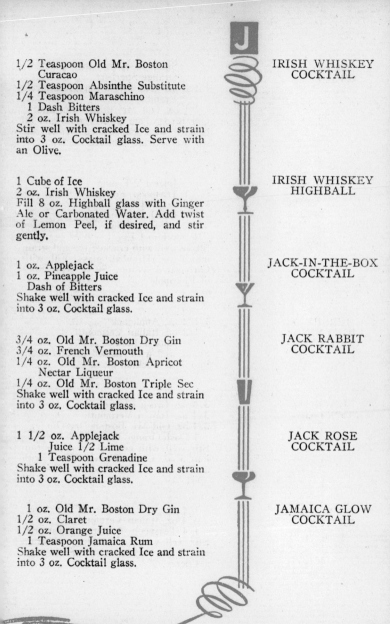

J

JAMAICA GRANITO

Small scoop of either Lemon or Orange Sherbert
1 1/2 oz. Old Mr. Boston California Brandy
1 oz. Old Mr. Boston Curacao
Use 12 oz. Tom Collins glass and fill balance with Carbonated Water and stir well. Grate Nutmeg on top.

JAPANESE FIZZ

Juice 1/2 Lemon
1 Teaspoon Powdered Sugar
1 1/2 oz. Old Mr. Boston Rye or Bourbon Whiskey
1/2 oz. Port Wine
White 1 Egg
Shake well with cracked Ice and strain into 8 oz. Highball glass. Fill with Carbonated Water. Serve with Slice of Pineapple.

JERSEY LIGHTNING COCKTAIL

1 1/2 oz. Applejack
1/2 oz. Italian Vermouth
Juice 1 Lime
Shake well with cracked Ice and strain into 3 oz. Cocktail glass.

JEWEL COCKTAIL

3/4 oz. Green Chartreuse
3/4 oz. Italian Vermouth
3/4 oz. Old Mr. Boston Dry Gin
1 Dash Orange Bitters
Stir well with cracked Ice and strain into 3 oz. Cocktail glass. Serve with a Cherry.

JEYPLAK COCKTAIL

1 1/2 oz. Old Mr. Boston Dry Gin
3/4 oz. Italian Vermouth
1/4 Teaspoon Absinthe Substitute
Stir well with cracked Ice and strain into 3 oz. Cocktail glass. Serve with a Cherry.

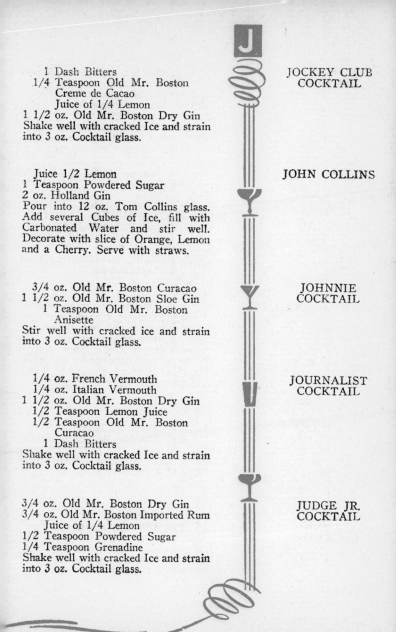

1 Dash Bitters
1/4 Teaspoon Old Mr. Boston
    Creme de Cacao
    Juice of 1/4 Lemon
1 1/2 oz. Old Mr. Boston Dry Gin
Shake well with cracked Ice and strain
into 3 oz. Cocktail glass.

JOCKEY CLUB COCKTAIL

Juice 1/2 Lemon
1 Teaspoon Powdered Sugar
2 oz. Holland Gin
Pour into 12 oz. Tom Collins glass.
Add several Cubes of Ice, fill with
Carbonated Water and stir well.
Decorate with slice of Orange, Lemon
and a Cherry. Serve with straws.

JOHN COLLINS

3/4 oz. Old Mr. Boston Curacao
1 1/2 oz. Old Mr. Boston Sloe Gin
1 Teaspoon Old Mr. Boston
    Anisette
Stir well with cracked ice and strain
into 3 oz. Cocktail glass.

JOHNNIE COCKTAIL

1/4 oz. French Vermouth
1/4 oz. Italian Vermouth
1 1/2 oz. Old Mr. Boston Dry Gin
1/2 Teaspoon Lemon Juice
1/2 Teaspoon Old Mr. Boston
    Curacao
1 Dash Bitters
Shake well with cracked Ice and strain
into 3 oz. Cocktail glass.

JOURNALIST COCKTAIL

3/4 oz. Old Mr. Boston Dry Gin
3/4 oz. Old Mr. Boston Imported Rum
    Juice of 1/4 Lemon
1/2 Teaspoon Powdered Sugar
1/4 Teaspoon Grenadine
Shake well with cracked Ice and strain
into 3 oz. Cocktail glass.

JUDGE JR. COCKTAIL

K

JUDGETTE
COCKTAIL

3/4 oz. Old Mr. Boston Peach
    Flavored Brandy
3/4 oz. Old Mr. Boston Dry Gin
3/4 oz. French Vermouth
    Juice of 1/4 Lime
Shake well with cracked Ice and strain
into 3 oz. Cocktail glass. Serve with
a Cherry.

JULEPS

See Index on page 14 for complete list
of Julep recipes.

JUPITER
COCKTAIL

    3/4 oz. French Vermouth
1 1/4 oz. Old Mr. Boston Dry Gin
    1 Teaspoon Orange Juice
    1 Teaspoon Old Mr. Boston
        Creme de Cacao
Shake well with cracked Ice and strain
into 3 oz. Cocktail glass.

K. C. B. COCKTAIL

    1/2 oz. Old Mr. Boston Kummel
1 1/2 oz. Old Mr. Boston Dry Gin
    1/4 Teaspoon Old Mr. Boston
        Apricot Flavored Brandy
    1/4 Teaspoon Lemon Juice
Shake well with cracked Ice and strain
into 3 oz. Cocktail glass. Add Twist
of Lemon Peel and drop in glass.

KENTUCKY
COCKTAIL

1 1/4 oz. Pineapple Juice
    3/4 oz. Old Mr. Boston Bourbon
        Whiskey
Shake well with cracked Ice and strain
into 3 oz. Cocktail glass.

KENTUCKY
COLONEL
COCKTAIL

    1/2 oz. Benedictine
1 1/2 oz. Old Mr. Boston Bourbon
        Whiskey
    Twist of Lemon Peel
Stir well with cracked Ice and strain
into a 3 oz. Cocktail glass.

K

1 Slice of Orange
1 Slice of Pineapple
1/2 Teaspoon Powdered Sugar
    Muddle well in Old Fashioned
    Cocktail glass and add:
2 oz. Old Mr. Boston Rye or
    Bourbon Whiskey
1 Cube of Ice
Stir well.

KING COLE COCKTAIL

3/4 oz. Old Mr. Boston Dry Gin
3/4 oz. Old Mr. Boston Wild Cherry
    Flavored Brandy
3/4 oz. French Vermouth
Stir well with cracked ice and strain
into 3 oz. Cocktail glass.

KISS-IN-THE-DARK COCKTAIL

Into 12 oz. Tom Collins glass, put:
1/2 Teaspoon Powdered Sugar
2 oz. Carbonated Water, and stir.
    Fill glass with cracked Ice and add:
2 oz. Old Mr. Boston Rye or
    Bourbon Whiskey.
    Fill with Carbonated Water or
    Ginger Ale
Insert Spiral of Orange or Lemon Peel
(or both) and dangle end over rim of
glass.

KLONDIKE COOLER

3/4 oz. French Vermouth
1 1/2 oz. Old Mr. Boston Dry Gin
1/4 Teaspoon Italian Vermouth
Stir well with cracked Ice and strain
into 3 oz. Cocktail glass. Add Twist
of Lemon Peel and drop in glass.

KNICKERBOCKER COCKTAIL

1 Teaspoon Raspberry Syrup
1 Teaspoon Lemon Juice
1 Teaspoon Orange Juice
2 oz. Old Mr. Boston Imported Rum
1/2 Teaspoon Old Mr. Boston Curacao
Shake well with cracked Ice and strain
into 4 oz. Cocktail glass. Decorate with
small slice of Pineapple.

KNICKERBOCKER SPECIAL COCKTAIL

L

KNOCK-OUT
COCKTAIL

1/2 oz. Absinthe Substitute
3/4 oz. Old Mr. Boston Dry Gin
3/4 oz. French Vermouth
1 Teaspoon Old Mr. Boston Creme
de Menthe (White)
Shake well with cracked Ice and strain
into 3 oz. Cocktail glass. Serve with
a Cherry.

KUP'S
INDISPENSABLE
COCKTAIL

1/2 oz. Italian Vermouth
1/2 oz. French Vermouth
1 1/4 oz. Old Mr. Boston Dry Gin
1 Dash Bitters
Stir well with cracked Ice and strain
into 3 oz. Cocktail glass.

LADIES' COCKTAIL

1 3/4 oz. Old Mr. Boston Rye or
Bourbon Whiskey
1/2 Teaspoon Absinthe Substitute
1/2 Teaspoon Old Mr. Boston
Anisette
2 Dashes Bitters
Shake well with cracked Ice and strain
into 3 oz. Cocktail glass. Serve with
a piece of Pineapple on top.

LADY LOVE FIZZ

1 Teaspoon Powdered Sugar
Juice of 1/2 Lemon
White of 1 Egg
2 oz. Old Mr. Boston Dry Gin
2 Teaspoons Sweet Cream
Shake well with cracked Ice and strain
into 8 oz. Highball glass. Fill with
Carbonated Water.

LASKY COCKTAIL

3/4 oz. Grape Juice
3/4 oz. Swedish Punch
3/4 oz. Old Mr. Boston Dry Gin
Shake well with cracked Ice and strain
into 3 oz. Cocktail glass.

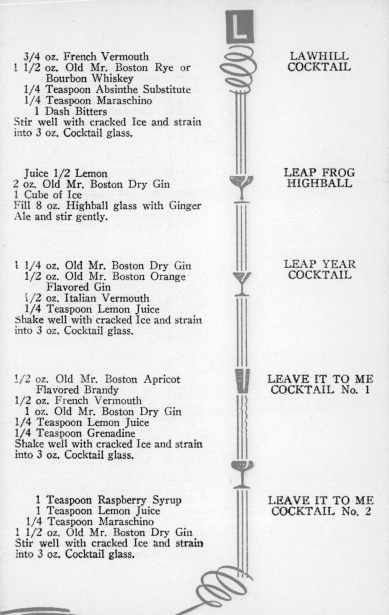

L

3/4 oz. French Vermouth
1 1/2 oz. Old Mr. Boston Rye or
    Bourbon Whiskey
1/4 Teaspoon Absinthe Substitute
1/4 Teaspoon Maraschino
    1 Dash Bitters
Stir well with cracked Ice and strain
into 3 oz. Cocktail glass.

**LAWHILL
COCKTAIL**

Juice 1/2 Lemon
2 oz. Old Mr. Boston Dry Gin
1 Cube of Ice
Fill 8 oz. Highball glass with Ginger
Ale and stir gently.

**LEAP FROG
HIGHBALL**

1 1/4 oz. Old Mr. Boston Dry Gin
1/2 oz. Old Mr. Boston Orange
    Flavored Gin
1/2 oz. Italian Vermouth
1/4 Teaspoon Lemon Juice
Shake well with cracked Ice and strain
into 3 oz. Cocktail glass.

**LEAP YEAR
COCKTAIL**

1/2 oz. Old Mr. Boston Apricot
    Flavored Brandy
1/2 oz. French Vermouth
1 oz. Old Mr. Boston Dry Gin
1/4 Teaspoon Lemon Juice
1/4 Teaspoon Grenadine
Shake well with cracked Ice and strain
into 3 oz. Cocktail glass.

**LEAVE IT TO ME
COCKTAIL No. 1**

1 Teaspoon Raspberry Syrup
1 Teaspoon Lemon Juice
1/4 Teaspoon Maraschino
1 1/2 oz. Old Mr. Boston Dry Gin
Stir well with cracked Ice and strain
into 3 oz. Cocktail glass.

**LEAVE IT TO ME
COCKTAIL No. 2**

LEMON SQUASH

1 Lemon, quartered
2 Teaspoons Powdered Sugar
Muddle well in 12 oz. Tom Collins
glass until juice is well extracted.
Then fill glass with cracked Ice and
fill with Carbonated Water and stir
well. Decorate with Fruits.

LEMONADE
(Carbonated)

Juice of 1 Lemon
2 Teaspoons Powdered Sugar
Fill 12 oz. Tom Collins glass with
shaved Ice. Add enough Carbonated
Water to fill glass and stir well.
Decorate with Slice of Orange, Lemon
and a Cherry. Serve with straws.

LEMONADE
(Claret)

Juice 1 Lemon
2 Teaspoons Powdered Sugar
Fill 12 oz. Tom Collins glass with
shaved Ice. Add enough water to fill
glass, leaving room to float 2 oz.
Claret. Decorate with a slice of
Orange, Lemon and a Cherry. Serve
with straws.

LEMONADE
(Egg)

Juice 1 Lemon
2 Teaspoons Powdered Sugar
1 Whole Egg
Shake well and strain into 12 oz.
Tom Collins glass filled with shaved
Ice. Add enough water to fill glass.
Serve with straws.

LEMONADE
(Fruit)

Juice 1 Lemon
2 Teaspoons Powdered Sugar
1 oz. Raspberry Syrup
Fill 12 oz. Tom Collins glass with
shaved Ice. Add enough water to fill
glass and stir well. Decorate with a
slice of Orange, Lemon and a Cherry.
Serve with straws.

Juice 1 Lemon
2 Teaspoons Powdered Sugar
Yolk of 1 Egg
6 oz. Water
Shake well with cracked Ice and strain into 12 oz. Tom Collins glass. Decorate with a slice of Orange, Lemon and a Cherry.

LEMONADE
(Golden)

2 Teaspoons Powdered Sugar
1 1/2 oz. Sherry Wine
1 oz. Old Mr. Boston Sloe Gin
Cut Lemon in quarters and muddle well with Sugar. Add Sherry and Sloe Gin. Shake well with cracked Ice and strain into 12 oz. Tom Collins glass. Fill glass with Carbonated Water.

LEMONADE
(Modern)

Juice 1 Lemon
2 Teaspoons Powdered Sugar
Fill 12 oz. Tom Collins glass with shaved Ice. Add enough water to fill glass and stir well. Decorate with a slice of Orange, Lemon and a Cherry. Serve with straws.

LEMONADE
(Plain)

3/4 oz. Old Mr. Boston Imported Rum
1 1/2 oz. Applejack
1/4 Teaspoon Simple Syrup
Stir well with cracked Ice and strain into 3 oz. Cocktail glass.

LIBERTY
COCKTAIL

Juice 3 Limes
3 Teaspoons Powdered Sugar
Fill 12 oz. Tom Collins glass with shaved Ice. Add enough water to fill glass. Stir well and drop Lime in glass. Add a Cherry. Serve with straws.

LIMEADE

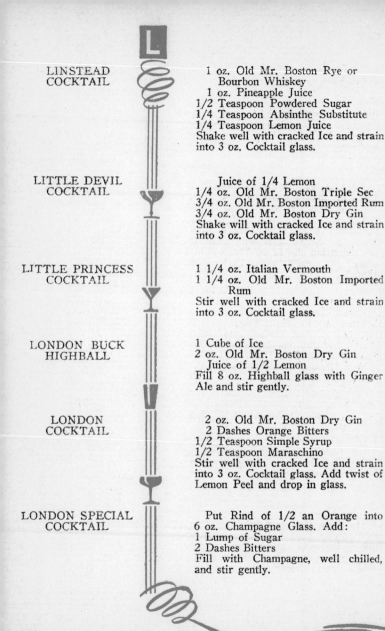

LINSTEAD COCKTAIL

1 oz. Old Mr. Boston Rye or
    Bourbon Whiskey
1 oz. Pineapple Juice
1/2 Teaspoon Powdered Sugar
1/4 Teaspoon Absinthe Substitute
1/4 Teaspoon Lemon Juice
Shake well with cracked Ice and strain
into 3 oz. Cocktail glass.

LITTLE DEVIL COCKTAIL

Juice of 1/4 Lemon
1/4 oz. Old Mr. Boston Triple Sec
3/4 oz. Old Mr. Boston Imported Rum
3/4 oz. Old Mr. Boston Dry Gin
Shake will with cracked Ice and strain
into 3 oz. Cocktail glass.

LITTLE PRINCESS COCKTAIL

1 1/4 oz. Italian Vermouth
1 1/4 oz. Old Mr. Boston Imported
    Rum
Stir well with cracked Ice and strain
into 3 oz. Cocktail glass.

LONDON BUCK HIGHBALL

1 Cube of Ice
2 oz. Old Mr. Boston Dry Gin
    Juice of 1/2 Lemon
Fill 8 oz. Highball glass with Ginger
Ale and stir gently.

LONDON COCKTAIL

2 oz. Old Mr. Boston Dry Gin
2 Dashes Orange Bitters
1/2 Teaspoon Simple Syrup
1/2 Teaspoon Maraschino
Stir well with cracked Ice and strain
into 3 oz. Cocktail glass. Add twist of
Lemon Peel and drop in glass.

LONDON SPECIAL COCKTAIL

Put Rind of 1/2 an Orange into
6 oz. Champagne Glass. Add:
1 Lump of Sugar
2 Dashes Bitters
Fill with Champagne, well chilled,
and stir gently.

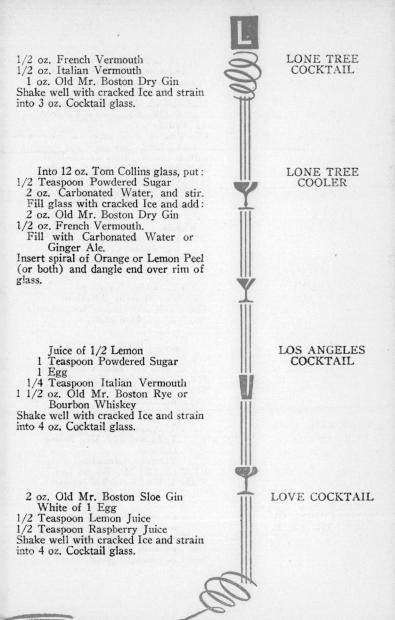

1/2 oz. French Vermouth
1/2 oz. Italian Vermouth
 1 oz. Old Mr. Boston Dry Gin
Shake well with cracked Ice and strain
into 3 oz. Cocktail glass.

LONE TREE COCKTAIL

   Into 12 oz. Tom Collins glass, put:
1/2 Teaspoon Powdered Sugar
 2 oz. Carbonated Water, and stir.
Fill glass with cracked Ice and add:
 2 oz. Old Mr. Boston Dry Gin
1/2 oz. French Vermouth.
   Fill with Carbonated Water or
      Ginger Ale.
Insert spiral of Orange or Lemon Peel
(or both) and dangle end over rim of
glass.

LONE TREE COOLER

   Juice of 1/2 Lemon
 1 Teaspoon Powdered Sugar
 1 Egg
1/4 Teaspoon Italian Vermouth
1 1/2 oz. Old Mr. Boston Rye or
      Bourbon Whiskey
Shake well with cracked Ice and strain
into 4 oz. Cocktail glass.

LOS ANGELES COCKTAIL

 2 oz. Old Mr. Boston Sloe Gin
   White of 1 Egg
1/2 Teaspoon Lemon Juice
1/2 Teaspoon Raspberry Juice
Shake well with cracked Ice and strain
into 4 oz. Cocktail glass.

LOVE COCKTAIL

LOVING CUP

Use large Glass Pitcher.
4 Teaspoons Powdered Sugar
6 oz. Carbonated Water
1/2 oz. Old Mr. Boston Triple Sec
1/2 oz. Old Mr. Boston Curacao
2 oz. Old Mr. Boston California
Brandy
Fill Pitcher with cubes of Ice. Add
1 Pint Claret. Stir well and decorate
with as many Fruits as available and
also Rind of Cucumber inserted on
each side of Pitcher. Top with small
bunch of Mint Sprigs.

LUXURY
COCKTAIL

3 oz. Old Mr. Boston California
Brandy
2 Dashes Orange Bitters
3 oz. well chilled Champagne
Use 6 oz. Saucer Champagne glass.

MACARONI
COCKTAIL

3/4 oz. Italian Vermouth
1 1/2 oz. Absinthe Substitute
Shake well with cracked Ice and strain
into 3 oz. Cocktail glass.

MAGNOLIA
BLOSSOM
COCKTAIL

Juice of 1/4 Lemon
1/2 oz. Sweet Cream
1 oz. Old Mr. Boston Dry Gin
1/4 Teaspoon Grenadine
Shake well with cracked Ice and strain
into 3 oz. Cocktail glass.

MAIDEN'S BLUSH
COCKTAIL No. 1

1/4 Teaspoon Lemon Juice
1 Teaspoon Old Mr. Boston
Curacao
1 Teaspoon Grenadine
1 1/2 oz. Old Mr. Boston Dry Gin
Shake well with cracked Ice and strain
into 3 oz. Cocktail glass.

MAIDEN'S BLUSH
COCKTAIL No. 2

3/4 oz. Absinthe Substitute
1 1/2 oz. Old Mr. Boston Dry Gin
1 Teaspoon Grenadine
Stir well with cracked Ice and strain
into 3 oz. Cocktail glass.

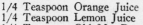

1/4 Teaspoon Orange Juice
1/4 Teaspoon Lemon Juice
1/4 Teaspoon Old Mr. Boston Triple Sec
2 oz. Old Mr. Boston Dry Gin
Shake well with cracked Ice and strain into 3 oz. Cocktail glass.

MAIDEN'S PRAYER COCKTAIL

3/4 oz. Old Mr. Boston Dry Gin
3/4 oz. Old Mr. Boston Triple Sec
3/4 oz. Grape Juice
Shake well with cracked Ice and strain into 3 oz. Cocktail glass.

MAINBRACE COCKTAIL

1/4 oz. Lime Juice
1/4 oz. Lemon Juice
1/2 Teaspoon Powdered Sugar
12 Mint Leaves
Muddle well and pour into 12 oz. Tom Collins glass filled with shaved Ice, and add: 2 oz. Old Mr. Boston Dry Gin. Stir gently, until glass is frosted. Decorate with Sprig of Mint and serve with straws.

MAJOR BAILEY

Juice 1/2 Lime
2 Cubes of Ice
2 oz. Scotch Whiskey
1 Dash Bitters
Fill 12 oz. Tom Collins glass with Carbonated Water and stir gently.

MAMIE GILROY

Juice 1/2 Lime
2 Cubes of Ice
2 oz. Scotch Whiskey
Fill 12 oz. Tom Collins glass with Ginger Ale and stir gently.

MAMIE TAYLOR

Juice 1 Lime, drop Skin in glass
2 Cubes of Ice
2 oz. Old Mr. Boston Dry Gin
Fill 12 oz. Tom Collins glass with Ginger Ale and stir gently.

MAMIE'S SISTER

MANHATTAN COCKTAIL

1 Dash Bitters
3/4 oz. Italian Vermouth
1 1/2 oz. Old Mr. Boston Rye or Bourbon Whiskey
Stir well with cracked Ice and strain into 3 oz. Cocktail glass. Serve with a Cherry.

MANHATTAN COCKTAIL (Dry)

1 Dash Bitters
3/4 oz. French Vermouth
1 1/2 oz. Old Mr. Boston Rye or Bourbon Whiskey
Stir well with cracked ice and strain into 3 oz. Cocktail glass. Serve with an Olive.

MANHATTAN COCKTAIL (Sweet)

1 Dash Bitters
1/4 Teaspoon Powdered Sugar
3/4 oz. Italian Vermouth
1 1/2 oz. Old Mr. Boston Rye or Bourbon Whiskey
Stir well with cracked Ice and strain into 3 oz. Cocktail glass. Serve with a Cherry.

MANILA FIZZ

2 oz. Old Mr. Boston Dry Gin
1 Egg
1 Teaspoon Powdered Sugar
2 oz. Sarsaparilla
Juice 1 Lime or 1/2 Lemon
Shake well with cracked Ice and strain into 10 oz. Pilsner glass.

MARGUERITE COCKTAIL

1 Dash Orange Bitters
3/4 oz. French Vermouth
1/4 Teaspoon Old Mr. Boston Curacao
1 1/2 oz. Old Mr. Boston Dry Gin
Stir well with cracked Ice and strain into 3 oz. Cocktail glass. Serve with an Olive.

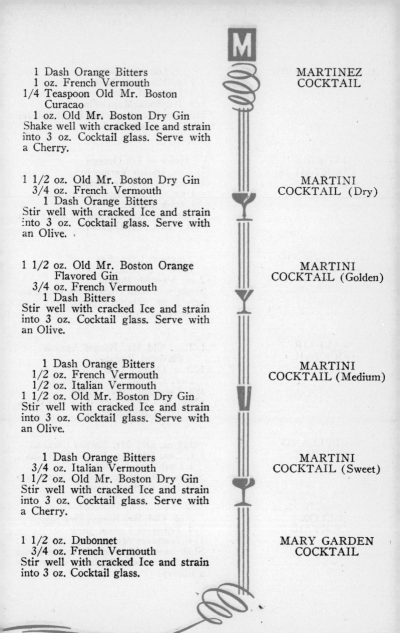

M

1 Dash Orange Bitters
1 oz. French Vermouth
1/4 Teaspoon Old Mr. Boston
    Curacao
1 oz. Old Mr. Boston Dry Gin
Shake well with cracked Ice and strain into 3 oz. Cocktail glass. Serve with a Cherry.

MARTINEZ
COCKTAIL

1 1/2 oz. Old Mr. Boston Dry Gin
3/4 oz. French Vermouth
1 Dash Orange Bitters
Stir well with cracked Ice and strain into 3 oz. Cocktail glass. Serve with an Olive.

MARTINI
COCKTAIL (Dry)

1 1/2 oz. Old Mr. Boston Orange
    Flavored Gin
3/4 oz. French Vermouth
1 Dash Bitters
Stir well with cracked Ice and strain into 3 oz. Cocktail glass. Serve with an Olive.

MARTINI
COCKTAIL (Golden)

1 Dash Orange Bitters
1/2 oz. French Vermouth
1/2 oz. Italian Vermouth
1 1/2 oz. Old Mr. Boston Dry Gin
Stir well with cracked Ice and strain into 3 oz. Cocktail glass. Serve with an Olive.

MARTINI
COCKTAIL (Medium)

1 Dash Orange Bitters
3/4 oz. Italian Vermouth
1 1/2 oz. Old Mr. Boston Dry Gin
Stir well with cracked Ice and strain into 3 oz. Cocktail glass. Serve with a Cherry.

MARTINI
COCKTAIL (Sweet)

1 1/2 oz. Dubonnet
3/4 oz. French Vermouth
Stir well with cracked Ice and strain into 3 oz. Cocktail glass.

MARY GARDEN
COCKTAIL

M

| MARY PICKFORD COCKTAIL | 1 oz. Old Mr. Boston Imported Rum
1 oz. Pineapple Juice
1/4 Teaspoon Grenadine
1/4 Teaspoon Maraschino
Shake well with cracked Ice and strain into 3 oz. Cocktail glass. |

| MAURICE COCKTAIL | Juice of 1/4 Orange
1/2 oz. Italian Vermouth
1/2 oz. French Vermouth
1 oz. Old Mr. Boston Dry Gin
1 Dash Bitters
Shake well with cracked Ice and strain into 4 oz. Cocktail glass. |

| MAY BLOSSOM FIZZ | 1 Teaspoon Grenadine
Juice 1/2 Lemon
2 oz. Swedish Punch
Shake well with cracked Ice and strain into 7 oz. Highball glass. Fill with Carbonated Water. |

| MAYFAIR COCKTAIL | 1/2 oz. Old Mr. Boston Apricot Flavored Brandy
1/2 oz. Orange Juice
1 oz. Old Mr. Boston Dry Gin
1/4 Teaspoon Clove Syrup
Shake well with cracked Ice and strain into 3 oz. Cocktail glass. |

| McCLELLAND COCKTAIL | 3/4 oz. Old Mr. Boston Curacao
1 1/2 oz. Old Mr. Boston Sloe Gin
1 Dash Orange Bitters
Shake well with cracked Ice and strain into 3 oz. Cocktail glass. |

| MELON COCKTAIL | 2 oz. Old Mr. Boston Dry Gin
1/4 Teaspoon Lemon Juice
1/4 Teaspoon Maraschino
Shake well with cracked Ice and strain into 3 oz. Cocktail glass. Serve with a Cherry. |

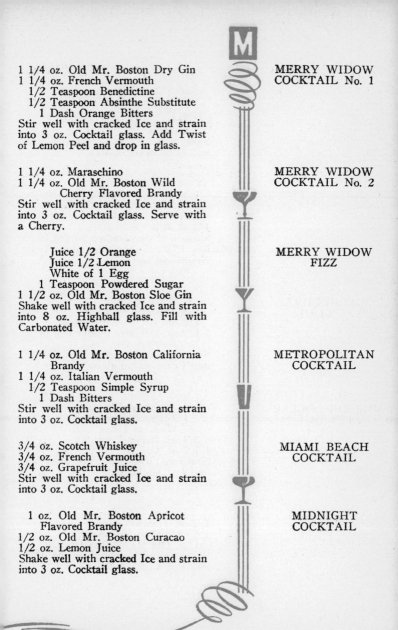

1 1/4 oz. Old **Mr.** Boston Dry Gin
1 1/4 oz. French Vermouth
  1/2 Teaspoon Benedictine
  1/2 Teaspoon Absinthe Substitute
   1 Dash Orange Bitters
Stir well with cracked Ice and strain
into 3 oz. Cocktail glass. Add Twist
of Lemon Peel and drop in glass.

**MERRY WIDOW
COCKTAIL No. 1**

1 1/4 oz. Maraschino
1 1/4 oz. Old **Mr.** Boston Wild
      Cherry Flavored Brandy
Stir well with cracked Ice and strain
into 3 oz. Cocktail glass. Serve with
a Cherry.

**MERRY WIDOW
COCKTAIL No. 2**

   Juice 1/2 Orange
   Juice 1/2 Lemon
   White of 1 Egg
   1 Teaspoon Powdered Sugar
1 1/2 oz. Old **Mr.** Boston Sloe Gin
Shake well with cracked Ice and strain
into 8 oz. Highball glass. Fill with
Carbonated Water.

**MERRY WIDOW
FIZZ**

1 1/4 oz. Old **Mr.** Boston California
      Brandy
1 1/4 oz. Italian Vermouth
  1/2 Teaspoon Simple Syrup
   1 Dash Bitters
Stir well with cracked Ice and strain
into 3 oz. Cocktail glass.

**METROPOLITAN
COCKTAIL**

3/4 oz. Scotch Whiskey
3/4 oz. French Vermouth
3/4 oz. Grapefruit Juice
Stir well with cracked Ice and strain
into 3 oz. Cocktail glass.

**MIAMI BEACH
COCKTAIL**

 1 oz. Old **Mr.** Boston Apricot
    Flavored Brandy
1/2 oz. Old **Mr.** Boston Curacao
1/2 oz. Lemon Juice
Shake well with cracked Ice and strain
into 3 oz. Cocktail glass.

**MIDNIGHT
COCKTAIL**

M

MIKADO COCKTAIL

2 oz. Old Mr. Boston California Brandy
2 Dashes Bitters
1/2 Teaspoon Old Mr. Boston Creme de Cacao
1/2 Teaspoon Old Mr. Boston Curacao
Shake well with cracked Ice and strain into 3 oz. Cocktail glass.

MILK PUNCH

1 Teaspoon Powdered Sugar
2 oz. Old Mr. Boston Rye or Bourbon Whiskey
1/2 pt. Milk
Shake well with cracked Ice and strain into 12 oz. Tom Collins glass. Grate Nutmeg on top.

MILLIONAIRE COCKTAIL

White of 1 Egg
1/4 Teaspoon Grenadine
1/2 oz. Mr. Boston Curacao
1 1/2 oz. Old Mr. Boston Rye or Bourbon Whiskey
Shake well with cracked Ice and strain into 4 oz. Cocktail glass.

MILLION DOLLAR COCKTAIL

2 Teaspoons Pineapple Juice
1 Teaspoon Grenadine
White of 1 Egg
3/4 oz. Italian Vermouth
1 1/2 oz. Old Mr. Boston Dry Gin
Shake well with cracked Ice and strain into 4 oz. Cocktail glass.

MINNEHAHA COCKTAIL

Juice of 1/4 Orange
1/2 oz. French Vermouth
1/2 oz. Italian Vermouth
1 oz. Old Mr. Boston Dry Gin
Shake well with cracked Ice and strain into 4 oz. Cocktail glass.

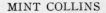

MINT COLLINS

Juice 1/2 Lemon
1 Teaspoon Powdered Sugar
2 oz. Old Mr. Boston Mint Flavored
Gin
Pour into 12 oz. Tom Collins glass.
Add several Cubes of Ice, fill with
Carbonated Water and stir well.
Decorate with slice of Lemon, Orange
and a Cherry. Serve with straws.

MINT HIGHBALL

1 Cube of Ice
2 oz. Old Mr. Boston Creme de
Menthe
Fill 8 oz. Highball glass with Ginger
Ale or Carbonated Water. Add twist
of Lemon Peel, if desired, and stir
gently.

MINT JULEP

Into Silver Mug or 12 oz. Tom
Collins glass put:
4 Sprigs of Mint
1 Teaspoon Powdered Sugar
2 Teaspoons of Water, and muddle.
Fill glass or mug with shaved Ice, add
2 1/2 oz. Old Mr. Boston Straight
Bourbon Whiskey, and stir gently until
glass is frosted. Decorate with slice of
Orange, Lemon, Pineapple and a
Cherry. Insert 5 or 6 Sprigs of Mint
on top. Serve with straws.

MINT JULEP
(Southern Style)

Fill silver mug or 12 oz. Tom Collins
glass with finely shaved Ice. Add 2 1/2
oz. Old Mr. Boston Bourbon Whiskey
and stir until glass is heavily frosted.
(Do not hold glass with hand while
stirring.) Add 1 Teaspoon Powdered
Sugar and fill balance with water, and
stir. Decorate with 5 or 6 Sprigs of
Fresh Mint so that the tops are about
2 inches above rim of mug or glass.
Use short straws so that it is necessary
to bury nose in Mint. The Mint is
intended for odor rather than taste.

M

MR. MANHATTAN COCKTAIL

Muddle Lump of Sugar and
4 Sprigs of Mint
1/4 Teaspoon Lemon Juice
1 Teaspoon Orange Juice
1 1/2 oz. Old **Mr.** Boston Dry Gin
Shake well with cracked Ice and strain
into 3 oz. Cocktail glass.

MODERN COCKTAIL

1 1/2 oz. Scotch Whiskey
1/2 Teaspoon Lemon Juice
1/4 Teaspoon Absinthe Substitute
1/2 Teaspoon Jamaica Rum
1 Dash Orange Bitters
Shake well with cracked Ice and strain
into 3 oz. Cocktail glass. Serve with
a Cherry.

MONTE CARLO IMPERIAL HIGHBALL

2 oz. Old **Mr.** Boston Dry Gin
1/2 oz. Old Mr. Boston Creme de
Menthe (White)
Juice 1/4 Lemon
Shake well with cracked Ice and strain
into 8 oz. Highball glass and fill glass
with Champagne.

MONTMARTRE COCKTAIL

1 1/4 oz. Old **Mr.** Boston Dry Gin
1/2 oz. Italian Vermouth
1/2 oz. Old Mr. Boston Triple Sec
Stir well with cracked Ice and strain
into 3 oz. Cocktail glass. Serve with
a Cherry.

MORNING COCKTAIL

1 oz. Old **Mr.** Boston California
Brandy
1 oz. French Vermouth
1/4 Teaspoon Old Mr. Boston Curacao
1/4 Teaspoon Maraschino
1/4 Teaspoon Absinthe Substitute
2 Dashes Orange Bitters
Stir well with cracked Ice and strain
into 3 oz. Cocktail glass. Serve with
a Cherry.

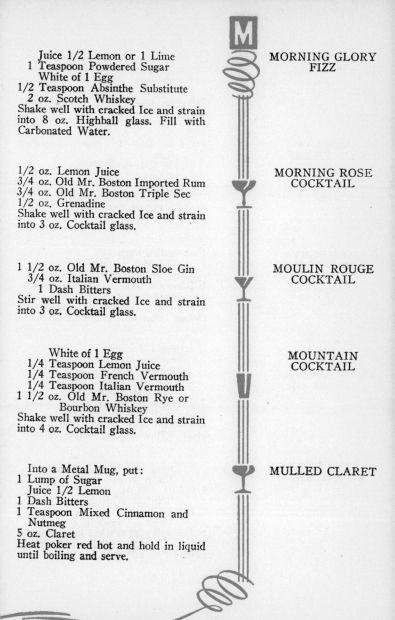

Juice 1/2 Lemon or 1 Lime
1 Teaspoon Powdered Sugar
  White of 1 Egg
1/2 Teaspoon Absinthe Substitute
  2 oz. Scotch Whiskey
Shake well with cracked Ice and strain into 8 oz. Highball glass. Fill with Carbonated Water.

MORNING GLORY FIZZ

1/2 oz. Lemon Juice
3/4 oz. Old Mr. Boston Imported Rum
3/4 oz. Old Mr. Boston Triple Sec
1/2 oz. Grenadine
Shake well with cracked Ice and strain into 3 oz. Cocktail glass.

MORNING ROSE COCKTAIL

1 1/2 oz. Old Mr. Boston Sloe Gin
  3/4 oz. Italian Vermouth
  1 Dash Bitters
Stir well with cracked Ice and strain into 3 oz. Cocktail glass.

MOULIN ROUGE COCKTAIL

White of 1 Egg
1/4 Teaspoon Lemon Juice
1/4 Teaspoon French Vermouth
1/4 Teaspoon Italian Vermouth
1 1/2 oz. Old Mr. Boston Rye or
          Bourbon Whiskey
Shake well with cracked Ice and strain into 4 oz. Cocktail glass.

MOUNTAIN COCKTAIL

Into a Metal Mug, put:
1 Lump of Sugar
  Juice 1/2 Lemon
1 Dash Bitters
1 Teaspoon Mixed Cinnamon and
  Nutmeg
5 oz. Claret
Heat poker red hot and hold in liquid until boiling and serve.

MULLED CLARET

**NAPOLEON
COCKTAIL**

2 oz. Old Mr. Boston Dry Gin
1/2 Teaspoon Old Mr. Boston
Curacao
1/2 Teaspoon Dubonnet
Stir well with cracked Ice and strain
into 3 oz. Cocktail glass.

**NEVADA
COCKTAIL**

1 1/2 oz. Old Mr. Boston Imported
Rum
1 oz. Grapefruit Juice
Juice of 1 Lime
1 Dash Bitters
3 Teaspoons Powdered Sugar
Shake well with cracked Ice and strain
into 4 oz. Cocktail glass.

**NEWBURY
COCKTAIL**

1 oz. Italian Vermouth
1 oz. Old Mr. Boston Dry Gin
Twist of Lemon Peel
1 Teaspoon Old Mr. Boston Curacao
Shake well with cracked Ice and strain
into 3 oz. Cocktail glass. Twist of
Orange Peel and drop in glass.

**NEW ORLEANS
GIN FIZZ**

Juice 1/2 Lemon
1 Teaspoon Powdered Sugar
White of 1 Egg
2 oz. Old Mr. Boston Dry Gin
1 Tablespoon Sweet Cream
1/2 Teaspoon Orange Flower Water
Shake extra well with cracked Ice
and strain into 12 oz. Tom Collins
glass. Fill with Carbonated Water.

**NEW YORK
COCKTAIL**

Juice 1 Lime or 1/2 Lemon
1 Teaspoon Powdered Sugar
1 1/2 oz. Old Mr. Boston Rye or
Bourbon Whiskey
1/2 Teaspoon Grenadine
Twist of Orange Peel
Shake well with cracked Ice and strain
into 3 oz. Cocktail glass. Add twist of
Lemon Peel and drop in glass.

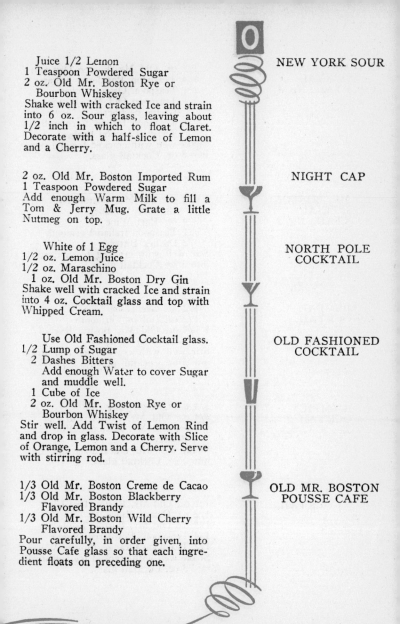

Juice 1/2 Lemon
1 Teaspoon Powdered Sugar
2 oz. Old Mr. Boston Rye or
  Bourbon Whiskey
Shake well with cracked Ice and strain into 6 oz. Sour glass, leaving about 1/2 inch in which to float Claret. Decorate with a half-slice of Lemon and a Cherry.

NEW YORK SOUR

2 oz. Old Mr. Boston Imported Rum
1 Teaspoon Powdered Sugar
Add enough Warm Milk to fill a Tom & Jerry Mug. Grate a little Nutmeg on top.

NIGHT CAP

White of 1 Egg
1/2 oz. Lemon Juice
1/2 oz. Maraschino
1 oz. Old Mr. Boston Dry Gin
Shake well with cracked Ice and strain into 4 oz. Cocktail glass and top with Whipped Cream.

NORTH POLE COCKTAIL

Use Old Fashioned Cocktail glass.
1/2 Lump of Sugar
2 Dashes Bitters
  Add enough Water to cover Sugar and muddle well.
1 Cube of Ice
2 oz. Old Mr. Boston Rye or
  Bourbon Whiskey
Stir well. Add Twist of Lemon Rind and drop in glass. Decorate with Slice of Orange, Lemon and a Cherry. Serve with stirring rod.

OLD FASHIONED COCKTAIL

1/3 Old Mr. Boston Creme de Cacao
1/3 Old Mr. Boston Blackberry
  Flavored Brandy
1/3 Old Mr. Boston Wild Cherry
  Flavored Brandy
Pour carefully, in order given, into Pousse Cafe glass so that each ingredient floats on preceding one.

OLD MR. BOSTON POUSSE CAFE

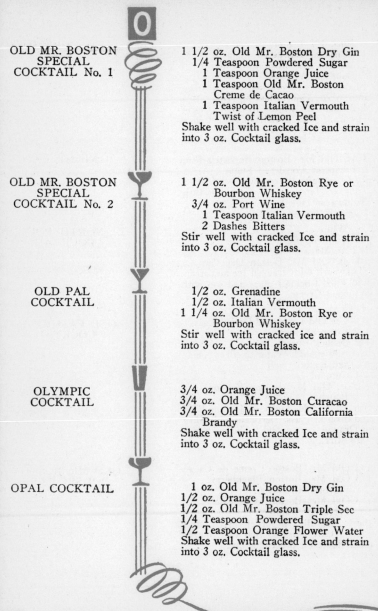

OLD MR. BOSTON SPECIAL COCKTAIL No. 1

1 1/2 oz. Old Mr. Boston Dry Gin
1/4 Teaspoon Powdered Sugar
1 Teaspoon Orange Juice
1 Teaspoon Old Mr. Boston Creme de Cacao
1 Teaspoon Italian Vermouth
Twist of Lemon Peel
Shake well with cracked Ice and strain into 3 oz. Cocktail glass.

OLD MR. BOSTON SPECIAL COCKTAIL No. 2

1 1/2 oz. Old Mr. Boston Rye or Bourbon Whiskey
3/4 oz. Port Wine
1 Teaspoon Italian Vermouth
2 Dashes Bitters
Stir well with cracked Ice and strain into 3 oz. Cocktail glass.

OLD PAL COCKTAIL

1/2 oz. Grenadine
1/2 oz. Italian Vermouth
1 1/4 oz. Old Mr. Boston Rye or Bourbon Whiskey
Stir well with cracked ice and strain into 3 oz. Cocktail glass.

OLYMPIC COCKTAIL

3/4 oz. Orange Juice
3/4 oz. Old Mr. Boston Curacao
3/4 oz. Old Mr. Boston California Brandy
Shake well with cracked Ice and strain into 3 oz. Cocktail glass.

OPAL COCKTAIL

1 oz. Old Mr. Boston Dry Gin
1/2 oz. Orange Juice
1/2 oz. Old Mr. Boston Triple Sec
1/4 Teaspoon Powdered Sugar
1/2 Teaspoon Orange Flower Water
Shake well with cracked Ice and strain into 3 oz. Cocktail glass.

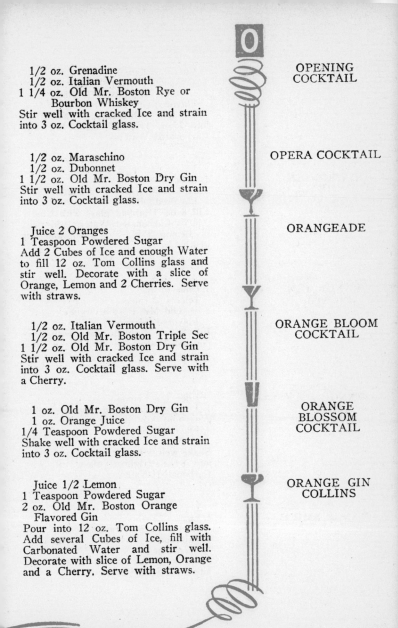

1/2 oz. Grenadine
1/2 oz. Italian Vermouth
1 1/4 oz. Old Mr. Boston Rye or
    Bourbon Whiskey
Stir well with cracked Ice and strain
into 3 oz. Cocktail glass.

OPENING COCKTAIL

1/2 oz. Maraschino
1/2 oz. Dubonnet
1 1/2 oz. Old Mr. Boston Dry Gin
Stir well with cracked Ice and strain
into 3 oz. Cocktail glass.

OPERA COCKTAIL

Juice 2 Oranges
1 Teaspoon Powdered Sugar
Add 2 Cubes of Ice and enough Water
to fill 12 oz. Tom Collins glass and
stir well. Decorate with a slice of
Orange, Lemon and 2 Cherries. Serve
with straws.

ORANGEADE

1/2 oz. Italian Vermouth
1/2 oz. Old Mr. Boston Triple Sec
1 1/2 oz. Old Mr. Boston Dry Gin
Stir well with cracked Ice and strain
into 3 oz. Cocktail glass. Serve with
a Cherry.

ORANGE BLOOM COCKTAIL

1 oz. Old Mr. Boston Dry Gin
1 oz. Orange Juice
1/4 Teaspoon Powdered Sugar
Shake well with cracked Ice and strain
into 3 oz. Cocktail glass.

ORANGE BLOSSOM COCKTAIL

Juice 1/2 Lemon
1 Teaspoon Powdered Sugar
2 oz. Old Mr. Boston Orange
    Flavored Gin
Pour into 12 oz. Tom Collins glass.
Add several Cubes of Ice, fill with
Carbonated Water and stir well.
Decorate with slice of Lemon, Orange
and a Cherry. Serve with straws.

ORANGE GIN COLLINS

ORANGE GIN FIZZ

Juice 1/2 Lemon
1 Teaspoon Powdered Sugar
2 oz. Old Mr. Boston Orange
Flavored Gin
Shake well with cracked Ice and strain into 7 oz. Highball glass. Fill with Carbonated Water.

ORANGE GIN HIGHBALL

1 Cube of Ice
2 oz. Old Mr. Boston Orange
Flavored Gin
Fill 8 oz. Highball glass with Ginger Ale or Carbonated Water. Add twist of Lemon Peel, if desired, and stir gently.

ORANGE GIN RICKEY

1 Cube of Ice
Juice 1/2 Lime
2 oz. Old Mr. Boston Orange
Flavored Gin
Fill 8 oz. Highball glass with Carbonated Water and stir. Leave Lime in glass.

ORANGE MILK FIZZ

Juice 1/2 Lemon
1 Teaspoon Powdered Sugar
2 oz. Old Mr. Boston Orange
Flavored Gin
2 oz. Milk
Shake well with cracked Ice and strain into 8 oz. Highball glass. Fill with Carbonated Water.

ORANGE SMILE

1 Egg
Juice 1 Large Orange
1 Tablespoon Raspberry Syrup or Grenadine
Shake well with cracked Ice and strain into 8 oz. Stem Goblet.

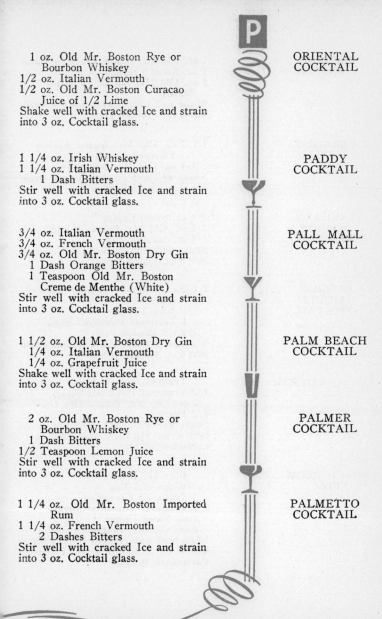

1 oz. Old Mr. Boston Rye or
    Bourbon Whiskey
1/2 oz. Italian Vermouth
1/2 oz. Old Mr. Boston Curacao
    Juice of 1/2 Lime
Shake well with cracked Ice and strain
into 3 oz. Cocktail glass.

ORIENTAL COCKTAIL

1 1/4 oz. Irish Whiskey
1 1/4 oz. Italian Vermouth
    1 Dash Bitters
Stir well with cracked Ice and strain
into 3 oz. Cocktail glass.

PADDY COCKTAIL

3/4 oz. Italian Vermouth
3/4 oz. French Vermouth
3/4 oz. Old Mr. Boston Dry Gin
    1 Dash Orange Bitters
    1 Teaspoon Old Mr. Boston
    Creme de Menthe (White)
Stir well with cracked Ice and strain
into 3 oz. Cocktail glass.

PALL MALL COCKTAIL

1 1/2 oz. Old Mr. Boston Dry Gin
    1/4 oz. Italian Vermouth
    1/4 oz. Grapefruit Juice
Shake well with cracked Ice and strain
into 3 oz. Cocktail glass.

PALM BEACH COCKTAIL

2 oz. Old Mr. Boston Rye or
    Bourbon Whiskey
    1 Dash Bitters
1/2 Teaspoon Lemon Juice
Stir well with cracked Ice and strain
into 3 oz. Cocktail glass.

PALMER COCKTAIL

1 1/4 oz. Old Mr. Boston Imported
    Rum
1 1/4 oz. French Vermouth
    2 Dashes Bitters
Stir well with cracked Ice and strain
into 3 oz. Cocktail glass.

PALMETTO COCKTAIL

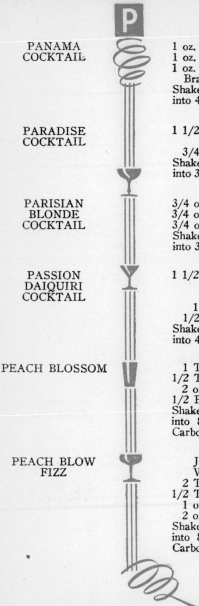

PANAMA COCKTAIL

1 oz. Old Mr. Boston Creme de Cacao
1 oz. Sweet Cream
1 oz. Old Mr. Boston California Brandy
Shake well with cracked Ice and strain into 4 oz. Cocktail glass.

PARADISE COCKTAIL

1 1/2 oz. Old Mr. Boston Apricot Flavored Brandy
3/4 oz. Old Mr. Boston Dry Gin
Shake well with cracked Ice and strain into 3 oz. Cocktail glass.

PARISIAN BLONDE COCKTAIL

3/4 oz. Sweet Cream
3/4 oz. Old Mr. Boston Curacao
3/4 oz. Jamaica Rum
Shake well with cracked Ice and strain into 3 oz. Cocktail glass.

PASSION DAIQUIRI COCKTAIL

1 1/2 oz. Old Mr. Boston Imported Rum
Juice 1 Lime
1 Teaspoon Powdered Sugar
1/2 oz. Passion Fruit
Shake well with cracked Ice and strain into 4 oz. Cocktail glass.

PEACH BLOSSOM

1 Teaspoon Lemon Juice
1/2 Teaspoon Powdered Sugar
2 oz. Old Mr. Boston Dry Gin
1/2 Peach
Shake well with cracked Ice and strain into 8 oz. Highball glass. Fill with Carbonated Water.

PEACH BLOW FIZZ

Juice 1/2 Lemon
White of 1 Egg
2 Teaspoons Grenadine
1/2 Teaspoon Powdered Sugar
1 oz. Sweet Cream
2 oz. Old Mr. Boston Dry Gin
Shake well with cracked Ice and strain into 8 oz. Highball glass. Fill with Carbonated Water.

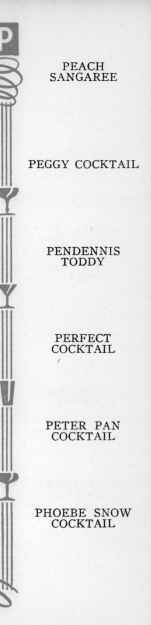

1 1/2 oz. Old Mr. Boston Peach
    Flavored Brandy
  1/2 Teaspoon Powdered Sugar
Shake well with cracked Ice and strain
into 3 oz. Cocktail glass, leaving
enough room on which to float a
Tablespoon of Port Wine.

PEACH SANGAREE

  3/4 oz. French Vermouth
1 1/2 oz. Old Mr. Boston Dry Gin
  1/4 Teaspoon Absinthe Substitute
  1/4 Teaspoon Dubonnet
Stir well with cracked Ice and strain
into 3 oz. Cocktail glass.

PEGGY COCKTAIL

Muddle Lump of Sugar with 1 Tea-
spoon of Water, in 6 oz. Sour glass.
Fill with finely shaved Ice, add 2 oz.
Old Mr. Boston Rye or Bourbon
Whiskey and stir well. Decorate with
2 slices of Lemon.

PENDENNIS TODDY

  1/4 oz. French Vermouth
  1/4 oz. Italian Vermouth
1 1/2 oz. Old Mr. Boston Dry Gin
  3 Dashes Bitters
Stir well with cracked Ice and strain
into 3 oz. Cocktail glass.

PERFECT COCKTAIL

  2 Dashes Bitters
3/4 oz. Orange Juice
3/4 oz. French Vermouth
3/4 oz. Old Mr. Boston Dry Gin
Shake well with cracked Ice and strain
into 3 oz. Cocktail glass.

PETER PAN COCKTAIL

1 1/4 oz. Dubonnet
1 1/4 oz. Old Mr. Boston California
    Brandy
  1/4 Teaspoon Absinthe Substitute
Stir well with cracked Ice and strain
into 3 oz. Cocktail glass.

PHOEBE SNOW COCKTAIL

PICCADILLY COCKTAIL

3/4 oz. French Vermouth
1 1/2 oz. Old Mr. Boston Dry Gin
1/4 Teaspoon Absinthe Substitute
1/4 Teaspoon Grenadine
Shake well with cracked Ice and strain into 3 oz. Cocktail glass.

PICK-ME-UP COCKTAIL

1 1/2 oz. Old Mr. Boston Apricot Flavored Brandy
1/2 oz. Lemon Juice
1 Teaspoon Grenadine
Shake well with cracked Ice and strain into 6 oz. Champagne glass, filling balance with Champagne.

PIKE'S PEAK COOLER

Juice 1/2 Lemon
1 Teaspoon Powdered Sugar
1 Egg
Shake well with cracked Ice and strain into 12 oz. Tom Collins glass and fill with Hard Cider.
Insert Spiral of Orange or Lemon Peel (or both) and dangle end over rim of glass.

PINEAPPLE COCKTAIL

3/4 oz. Pineapple Juice
1 1/2 oz. Old Mr. Boston Imported Rum
1/2 Teaspoon Lemon Juice
Shake well with cracked Ice and strain into 3 oz. Cocktail glass.

PINEAPPLE COOLER

Into 12 oz. Tom Collins glass, put:
1/2 Teaspoon Powdered Sugar
2 oz. Carbonated Water, and stir.
Fill glass with cracked Ice and add:
2 oz. Dry White Wine.
Fill with Carbonated Water.
Insert Spiral of Orange or Lemon Peel (or both) and dangle end over rim of glass.

BECOME A PERFECT HOST
in 12 Easy Lessons

Here are the twelve most popular mixed drinks.
The perfect host should know them all—and they
are all he really needs to know to please his guests.

Manhattan

Each serving requires ¾ ounce Italian Vermouth, 1½ ounces Old Mr. Boston Rye or Bourbon Whiskey and a dash of Bitters. Stir well in a mixing glass with a few pieces of Cracked Ice. Strain into 3 ounce Cocktail Glass and drop in a Cherry. *The pre-dinner cocktail par excellence.*

Old Fashioned

Muddle half a lump of Sugar with 2 dashes of Bitters and enough water to cover in an Old Fashioned Cocktail glass. Add a cube of ice and 2 ounces Old Mr. Boston Rye or Bourbon Whiskey and stir well. Twist a Lemon Rind for the drop of oil, add a slice of Lemon and a Cherry. Cut slice of Orange over the brim and serve with a stirring rod. *The time-tried favorite.*

Tom Collins

Squeeze the juice of half a lemon over a teaspoonful of Powdered Sugar in a 12 ounce glass—add 2 ounces Old Mr. Boston Dry Gin and several ice cubes. Fill glass with carbonated water and stir well. Drop in a Cherry and a slice of Lemon, cut half a slice of Orange over the brim of the glass and serve with straws. *Deservedly, the old reliable summer cooler.*

Sloe Gin Fizz

Shake 2 ounces Old Mr. Boston Sloe Gin with the juice of half a
Lemon, a Teaspoon of Powdered Sugar and Cracked Ice. Strain
into an 8 ounce Highball Glass, fill with Carbonated Water and
cut a slice of Lemon over the brim of the glass. *A foamy, tangy, thirst
quencher—always a favorite.*

Dry Martini

Put 1½ ounces Old Mr. Boston Dry Gin, ¾ ounce French Vermouth and a dash of Orange Bitters into a mixing glass—additional servings in the same proportions. Stir well with Cracked Ice, strain into 3 ounce Cocktail Glass and drop in an Olive. *The most popular American Appetizer.*

Cuba Libre

Squeeze half a Lime and drop the skin into 10 ounce glass. Add 2 ounces Old Mr. Boston Imported Rum and two cubes of Ice. Fill the glass with Cola and stir—*then you'll know why Havana Holidays are so intriguing.*

HORS D'OEUVRES AND CANAPES

1. *Roquefort Cheese Canapes*

Mash 1 (3-ounce) package cream cheese; combine with 1¼-ounce package of American Blue or Roquefort cheese, 2 teaspoons finely chopped onion, dash salt, and enough cream to moisten. Pile lightly on 12 toasted and buttered circles of bread with pastry tube or fork, leaving a narrow edge of toast showing around edge. Cut small circles from pimiento, and stick into top of cheese in petal fashion as shown.

1

2. *Rolled Crabmeat Sandwiches*

Combine 1 cup flaked cooked crabmeat, ¼ cup mixed pickle relish, dash of salt and pepper, and ¼ cup mayonnaise. Remove crusts from 12 thin slices bread; spread with butter and filling. Roll each as for jelly roll. Tuck small sprigs of watercress along edge of roll as shown. Fasten with toothpick. Wrap in waxed paper or damp towel. Chill at least ½ hour before serving.

2

3. *Smoked Salmon Canapes*

Blend ¼ cup softened butter, ½ teaspoon finely chopped chives, and 2 tablespoons finely chopped celery. Spread lightly on 12 plain buttered or toasted, star-shaped bread slices. Cut thin slices of smoked salmon into 12 small stars, and place on top as shown. Outline edges with finely chopped parsley.

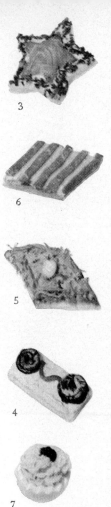

3

4. *Anchovy Canapes*

Mash 1 (3-ounce) package cream cheese; stir in 1 teaspoon lemon juice, ½ teaspoon chopped parsley, and enough cream to moisten. Spread lightly on 12 plain buttered or toasted rectangles of bread. Arrange 24 anchovies and 12 pimiento strips on top as shown.

6

5. *Chicken & Carrot Canapes*

Combine ½ cup finely ground cooked chicken with a dash of salt, a few drops each of lemon juice and Worcestershire sauce, 1 tablespoon chopped sweet pickle, and 4 tablespoons mayonnaise. Spread lightly on 12 plain buttered or toasted diamond-shaped bread slices. Sprinkle salted shredded carrots on edges as shown. Garnish center of each canape with ¼ teaspoon mayonnaise.

5

6. *Ham Canapes*

Blend ¼ pound softened yellow cheese, 1½ tablespoons cream, ¼ teaspoon mustard, dash of cayenne, and a few drops each of Worcestershire Sauce and vinegar. Spread lightly on 12 plain buttered or toasted rectangles of bread. Cut a thin slice of ham into short julienne strips, and arrange on each canape as shown.

4

7. *Deviled Egg Cups*

Hard cook and shell 12 eggs. To make cups: Cut through whites around center of egg making cuts in saw-tooth fashion with a sharp-pointed paring knife. Pull halves apart gently, and remove yolks. Mash yolks; blend with dash of salt and pepper, ⅛ teaspoon horseradish, ½ teaspoon lemon juice and enough mayonnaise to moisten. Pile lightly in whites, and top with caviar, if desired.

7

8. *Broiled Bacon Appetizers*

Wrap narrow strips of bacon around an assortment of the following: seasoned and cooked whole shrimp, cooked pitted prunes, halves of canned apricots; sprinkled with few drops of lemon juice before wrapping. Also wrap large stuffed olives, large pitted ripe olives, small cocktail sausages, pickled onions. Allow strips of bacon to lap lightly, and secure each with a toothpick. Broil until bacon is crisp.

8

Whiskey Sour

Squeeze half a lemon into a Cocktail Shaker with ½ teaspoon of Powdered Sugar, 2 ounces of Old Mr. Boston Rye or Bourbon Whiskey and a few pieces of Cracked Ice—shake well—strain into a 6 ounce Sour Glass and fill with Carbonated Water. Cut a slice of Lemon over the brim and drop in a Cherry—*a freshener whatever the weather may be.*

Golden Martini

Put 1½ ounces Old Mr. Boston Orange Flavored Gin, ¾ ounce French Vermouth, a dash of Bitters and a few pieces of Cracked Ice into a mixing glass—stir well—strain into 3 ounce Cocktail Glass and drop in an Olive—*a taste sensation that always pleases*.

Mint Julep (SOUTHERN STYLE)

Fill a 12 ounce glass with finely shaved ice, pour in 2½ ounces Old
Mr. Boston Bourbon Whiskey and stir until glass is heavily frosted.
Hold the glass lightly near the rim so that the heat of the hand will
not prevent frosting. Then add 1 Teaspoon Powdered Sugar, fill
with water and stir. Put in a few sprigs of fresh Mint and serve with
short straws so that the mint aroma will be inhaled when drinking.
The aristocratic drink of the Old South.

Rum Collins

Put the juice of 1 Lime, 1 Teaspoon of Powdered Sugar, 2 ounces Old Mr. Boston Imported Rum and several Cubes of Ice into a 12 ounce glass. Fill glass with Carbonated Water and stir well. Then cut a slice of Lemon on the brim, drop in a Cherry and the squeezed Lime and serve with straws. *An interesting variation of the Tom Collins.*

Daiquiri

For each serving use the juice of 1 Lime, 1 Teaspoon of Powdered Sugar and 1½ ounces Old Mr. Boston Imported Rum. Shake well with a few pieces of Cracked Ice in a Cocktail Shaker and strain into 3 ounce Cocktail Glass. *Then you'll know why the South American way is so appealing.*

Mint Collins

Squeeze ½ a Lemon into a tall 12 ounce glass—add 1 Teaspoon of Powdered Sugar, 2 ounces Old Mr. Boston Mint Flavored Gin and a few Cubes of Ice—fill with Carbonated Water and stir well. Drop in a slice of Lemon, a Cherry, cut a slice of Orange over the brim and serve with straws. *A tall drink that is just as cool as it looks.*

Old Mr. BOSTON

Importer and Distiller of

**FINE WHISKEYS AND GINS, BRANDIES,
RUMS AND LIQUEURS**

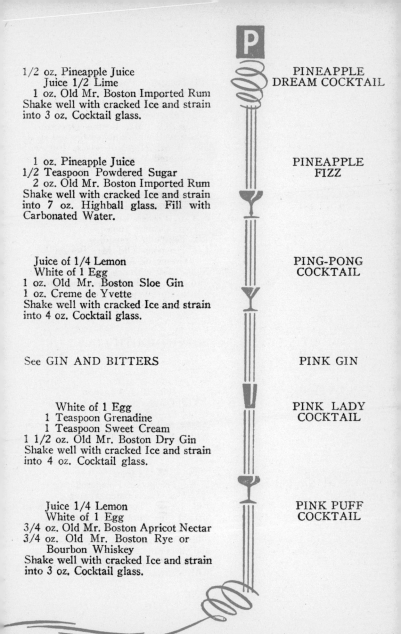

1/2 oz. Pineapple Juice
    Juice 1/2 Lime
  1 oz. Old Mr. Boston Imported Rum
Shake well with cracked Ice and strain
into 3 oz. Cocktail glass.

**PINEAPPLE
DREAM COCKTAIL**

  1 oz. Pineapple Juice
1/2 Teaspoon Powdered Sugar
  2 oz. Old Mr. Boston Imported Rum
Shake well with cracked Ice and strain
into 7 oz. Highball glass. Fill with
Carbonated Water.

**PINEAPPLE
FIZZ**

  Juice of 1/4 Lemon
  White of 1 Egg
1 oz. Old Mr. Boston Sloe Gin
1 oz. Creme de Yvette
Shake well with cracked Ice and strain
into 4 oz. Cocktail glass.

**PING-PONG
COCKTAIL**

See GIN AND BITTERS

PINK GIN

  White of 1 Egg
  1 Teaspoon Grenadine
  1 Teaspoon Sweet Cream
1 1/2 oz. Old Mr. Boston Dry Gin
Shake well with cracked Ice and strain
into 4 oz. Cocktail glass.

**PINK LADY
COCKTAIL**

  Juice 1/4 Lemon
  White of 1 Egg
3/4 oz. Old Mr. Boston Apricot Nectar
3/4 oz. Old Mr. Boston Rye or
    Bourbon Whiskey
Shake well with cracked Ice and strain
into 3 oz. Cocktail glass.

**PINK PUFF
COCKTAIL**

PINK ROSE FIZZ

Juice 1/2 Lemon
1 Teaspoon Powdered Sugar
White of 1 Egg
1/2 Teaspoon Grenadine
2 Teaspoons Sweet Cream
2 oz. Old Mr. Boston Dry Gin
Shake well with cracked Ice and strain into 8 oz. Highball glass. Fill with Carbonated Water.

PINK WHISKERS COCKTAIL

3/4 oz. Old Mr. Boston Apricot
Flavored Brandy
3/4 oz. French Vermouth
1 oz. Orange Juice
1 Teaspoon Grenadine
1/4 Teaspoon Old Mr. Boston
Creme de Menthe (White)
Shake well with cracked Ice and strain into 4 oz. Cocktail glass and top with a little Port Wine.

PLAIN VERMOUTH COCKTAIL

See VERMOUTH COCKTAIL

PLANTER'S COCKTAIL

Juice of 1/4 Lemon
1/2 Teaspoon Powdered Sugar
1 1/2 oz. Jamaica Rum
Shake well with cracked Ice and strain into 3 oz. Cocktail glass.

PLANTER'S PUNCH No. 1

Juice 2 Limes
2 Teaspoons Powdered Sugar
2 oz. Carbonated Water
Fill 12 oz. Tom Collins glass with shaved Ice and stir until glass is frosted. Add 2 Dashes Bitters. 2 1/2 oz. Old Mr. Boston Imported Rum. Stir and decorate with slice of Lemon, Orange, Pineapple and a Cherry. Serve with straws.

PLANTER'S PUNCH No. 2

Juice 1 Lime
Juice 1/2 Lemon
Juice 1/2 Orange
1 Teaspoon Pineapple Juice
2 oz. Old Mr. Boston Imported Rum
Pour above into 16 oz. glass, well filled with shaved Ice. Stir until glass is frosted. Then add 1 oz. Jamaica Rum and top with 1/4 Teaspoon Old Mr. Boston Curacao. Decorate with slice of Orange, Lemon, Pineapple and a Cherry, also Sprig of Mint dipped in Powdered Sugar. Serve with straws.

PLAZA COCKTAIL

3/4 oz. Italian Vermouth
3/4 oz. French Vermouth
3/4 oz. Old Mr. Boston Dry Gin
1 Strip of Pineapple
Shake well with cracked Ice and strain into 3 oz. Cocktail glass.

POKER COCKTAIL

1 1/4 oz. Italian Vermouth
1 1/4 oz. Old Mr. Boston Imported Rum
Stir well with cracked Ice and strain into 3 oz. Cocktail glass.

POLLYANNA COCKTAIL

Muddle 3 slices of Orange and 3 slices of Pineapple
2 oz. Old Mr. Boston Dry Gin
1/2 oz. Italian Vermouth
1/2 Teaspoon Grenadine
Shake well with cracked Ice and strain into 4 oz. Cocktail glass.

POLO COCKTAIL

1/2 oz. Lemon Juice
1/2 oz. Orange Juice
1 oz. Old Mr. Boston Dry Gin
Shake well with cracked Ice and strain into 3 oz. Cocktail glass.

115

**POOP DECK
COCKTAIL**

1 1/4 oz. Old Mr. Boston Blackberry
    Flavored Brandy
1/2 oz. Port Wine
1/2 oz. Old Mr. Boston California
    Brandy
Stir well with cracked Ice and strain
into 3 oz. Cocktail glass.

POPPY COCKTAIL

3/4 oz. Old Mr. Boston Creme de
    Cacao
1 1/2 oz. Old Mr. Boston Dry Gin
Shake well with cracked Ice and strain
into 3 oz. Cocktail glass.

**PORT AND
STARBOARD**

1/2 oz. Grenadine
1/2 oz. Old Mr. Boston Green
    Creme de Menthe
Pour carefully, in order given, into
Pousse Cafe glass, so that each
ingredient floats on preceding one.

**PORT MILK
PUNCH**

1 Teaspoon Powdered Sugar
3 oz. Port Wine
1/2 pt. Milk
Shake well with cracked Ice, strain
into 12 oz. Tom Collins glass and
grate Nutmeg on top.

**PORT WINE
COBBLER**

1 Teaspoon Powdered Sugar
2 oz. Carbonated Water
    Fill 8 oz. Goblet with shaved Ice
    Add 3 oz. Port Wine
Stir well and decorate with fruits in
season. Serve with straws.

**PORT WINE
COCKTAIL**

2 1/4 oz. Port Wine
1/2 Teaspoon Old Mr. Boston
    California Brandy
Stir slightly with cracked Ice and
strain into 3 oz. Cocktail glass.

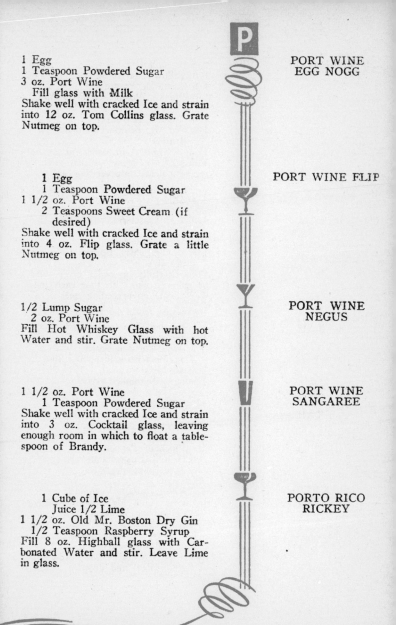

1 Egg
1 Teaspoon Powdered Sugar
3 oz. Port Wine
  Fill glass with Milk
Shake well with cracked Ice and strain into 12 oz. Tom Collins glass. Grate Nutmeg on top.

PORT WINE EGG NOGG

  1 Egg
  1 Teaspoon Powdered Sugar
1 1/2 oz. Port Wine
  2 Teaspoons Sweet Cream (if desired)
Shake well with cracked Ice and strain into 4 oz. Flip glass. Grate a little Nutmeg on top.

PORT WINE FLIP

1/2 Lump Sugar
  2 oz. Port Wine
Fill Hot Whiskey Glass with hot Water and stir. Grate Nutmeg on top.

PORT WINE NEGUS

1 1/2 oz. Port Wine
  1 Teaspoon Powdered Sugar
Shake well with cracked Ice and strain into 3 oz. Cocktail glass, leaving enough room in which to float a tablespoon of Brandy.

PORT WINE SANGAREE

  1 Cube of Ice
    Juice 1/2 Lime
1 1/2 oz. Old Mr. Boston Dry Gin
  1/2 Teaspoon Raspberry Syrup
Fill 8 oz. Highball glass with Carbonated Water and stir. Leave Lime in glass.

PORTO RICO RICKEY

POUSSE CAFE

1/6 Grenadine
1/6 Yellow Chartreuse
1/6 Creme de Yvette
1/6 Old Mr. Boston Creme de Menthe
(White)
1/6 Green Chartreuse
1/6 Old Mr. Boston California
Brandy

Pour carefully, in order given, into Pousse Cafe glass so that each ingredient floats on preceding one.

See Index on page 14 for complete list of Pousse Cafe recipes.

POUSSE L'AMOUR

1/3 oz. Maraschino
Yolk of 1 Egg
1/3 oz. Benedictine
1/3 oz. Old Mr. Boston California
Brandy

Pour carefully, in order given, into 2 oz. Sherry glass, so that each ingredient floats on preceding one.

**PRAIRIE HEN
COCKTAIL**

1 Whole Egg
1 Teaspoon Worcestershire Sauce
1/2 Teaspoon Vinegar
1 Drop Tobasco Sauce
Season with a little Salt and Pepper

Use 5 oz. Delmonico glass.

**PRAIRIE OYSTER
COCKTAIL**

1 Whole Egg
1 Teaspoon Worcestershire Sauce
1 Teaspoon Tomato Catsup
1/2 Teaspoon Vinegar
Pinch of Pepper
1 Drop Tabasco Sauce

Use 5 oz. Delmonico glass.

**PREAKNESS
COCKTAIL**

3/4 oz. Italian Vermouth
1 1/2 oz. Old Mr. Boston Rye or
Bourbon Whiskey
1 Dash Bitters
1/2 Teaspoon Benedictine

Shake well with cracked Ice and strain into 3 oz. Cocktail Glass. Add Twist of Lemon Peel and drop in glass.

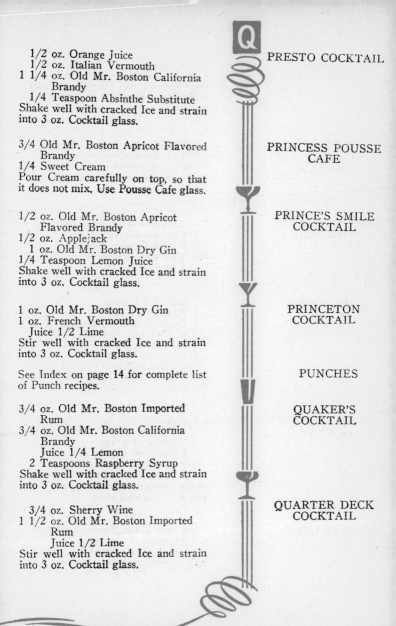

1/2 oz. Orange Juice
1/2 oz. Italian Vermouth
1 1/4 oz. Old Mr. Boston California
    Brandy
1/4 Teaspoon Absinthe Substitute
Shake well with cracked Ice and strain
into 3 oz. Cocktail glass.

PRESTO COCKTAIL

3/4 Old Mr. Boston Apricot Flavored
    Brandy
1/4 Sweet Cream
Pour Cream carefully on top, so that
it does not mix. Use Pousse Cafe glass.

PRINCESS POUSSE CAFE

1/2 oz. Old Mr. Boston Apricot
    Flavored Brandy
1/2 oz. Applejack
  1 oz. Old Mr. Boston Dry Gin
1/4 Teaspoon Lemon Juice
Shake well with cracked Ice and strain
into 3 oz. Cocktail glass.

PRINCE'S SMILE COCKTAIL

1 oz. Old Mr. Boston Dry Gin
1 oz. French Vermouth
    Juice 1/2 Lime
Stir well with cracked Ice and strain
into 3 oz. Cocktail glass.

PRINCETON COCKTAIL

See Index on page 14 for complete list
of Punch recipes.

PUNCHES

3/4 oz. Old Mr. Boston Imported
    Rum
3/4 oz. Old Mr. Boston California
    Brandy
    Juice 1/4 Lemon
  2 Teaspoons Raspberry Syrup
Shake well with cracked Ice and strain
into 3 oz. Cocktail glass.

QUAKER'S COCKTAIL

3/4 oz. Sherry Wine
1 1/2 oz. Old Mr. Boston Imported
    Rum
    Juice 1/2 Lime
Stir well with cracked Ice and strain
into 3 oz. Cocktail glass.

QUARTER DECK COCKTAIL

R

QUEEN
CHARLOTTE

2 oz. Claret
1 oz. Raspberry Syrup or Grenadine
Pour into 12 oz. Tom Collins glass.
Add cube of Ice, fill with Lemon Soda
and stir.

QUEEN
ELIZABETH
COCKTAIL

1 1/2 oz. Old Mr. Boston Dry Gin
1/2 oz. French Vermouth
1/4 oz. Benedictine
Stir well with cracked Ice and strain
into 3 oz. Cocktail glass.

RACQUET CLUB
COCKTAIL

1 1/2 oz. Old Mr. Boston Dry Gin
3/4 oz. French Vermouth
1 Dash Orange Bitters
Stir well with cracked Ice and strain
into 3 oz. Cocktail glass.

RAMOS FIZZ

Juice 1/2 Lemon
White of 1 Egg
1 Teaspoon Powdered Sugar
2 oz. Old Mr. Boston Dry Gin
1 Tablespoon Sweet Cream
1/2 Teaspoon Orange Flower Water
Shake extra well with cracked Ice and
strain into 12 oz. Tom Collins glass.
Fill with Carbonated Water.

RATTLESNAKE
COCKTAIL

1 1/2 oz. Old Mr. Boston Rye or
Bourbon Whiskey
White of 1 Egg
1 Teaspoon Lemon Juice
1/2 Teaspoon Powdered Sugar
1/4 Teaspoon Absinthe Substitute
Shake well with cracked Ice and strain
into 4 oz. Cocktail glass.

RED SWIZZLE

Made same as Gin Swizzle and add
1 Tablespoon of Grenadine.
If desired, Rum, Brandy or Whiskey
may be substituted for the Gin.

REFORM COCKTAIL

3/4 oz. French Vermouth
1 1/2 oz. Sherry Wine
1 Dash Orange Bitters
Stir well with cracked Ice and strain into 3 oz. Cocktail glass. Serve with a Cherry.

REMSEN COOLER

Into 12 oz. Tom Collins glass, put:
1/2 Teaspoon Powdered Sugar
  2 oz. Carbonated Water, and stir
    Fill glass with Cracked Ice and add:
  2 oz. Old Mr. Boston Dry Gin
    Fill with Carbonated Water or Ginger Ale
Insert spiral of Orange or Lemon Peel (or both) and dangle end over rim of glass.

RESOLUTE COCKTAIL

Juice 1/4 Lemon
1/2 oz. Old Mr. Boston Apricot Flavored Brandy
  1 oz. Old Mr. Boston Dry Gin
Shake well with cracked Ice and strain into 3 oz. Cocktail glass.

RHINE WINE CUP

Use Large Glass Pitcher
  4 Teaspoons Powdered Sugar
  6 oz. Carbonated Water
1/2 oz. Old Mr. Boston Triple Sec
1/2 oz. Old Mr. Boston Curacao
  2 oz. Old Mr. Boston California Brandy
Fill pitcher with cubes of Ice. Add 1 pint of Rhine Wine. Stir well and decorate with as many fruits as available and also Rind of Cucumber inserted on each side of pitcher. Top with small bunch of Mint Sprigs. Serve in 5 oz. Claret glass.

RICKIES

See Index on page 14 for complete list of Rickey recipes.

121

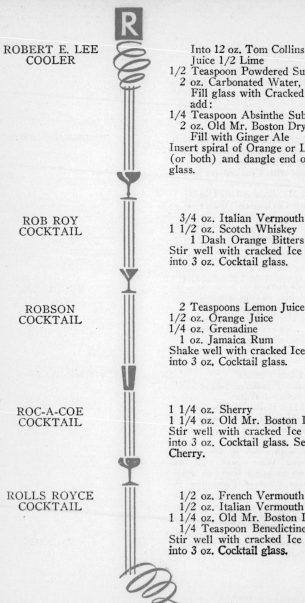

ROBERT E. LEE COOLER

Into 12 oz. Tom Collins glass, put:
Juice 1/2 Lime
1/2 Teaspoon Powdered Sugar
2 oz. Carbonated Water, and stir
Fill glass with Cracked Ice and add:
1/4 Teaspoon Absinthe Substitute
2 oz. Old Mr. Boston Dry Gin
Fill with Ginger Ale
Insert spiral of Orange or Lemon Peel (or both) and dangle end over rim of glass.

ROB ROY COCKTAIL

3/4 oz. Italian Vermouth
1 1/2 oz. Scotch Whiskey
1 Dash Orange Bitters
Stir well with cracked Ice and strain into 3 oz. Cocktail glass.

ROBSON COCKTAIL

2 Teaspoons Lemon Juice
1/2 oz. Orange Juice
1/4 oz. Grenadine
1 oz. Jamaica Rum
Shake well with cracked Ice and strain into 3 oz. Cocktail glass.

ROC-A-COE COCKTAIL

1 1/4 oz. Sherry
1 1/4 oz. Old Mr. Boston Dry Gin
Stir well with cracked Ice and strain into 3 oz. Cocktail glass. Serve with a Cherry.

ROLLS ROYCE COCKTAIL

1/2 oz. French Vermouth
1/2 oz. Italian Vermouth
1 1/4 oz. Old Mr. Boston Dry Gin
1/4 Teaspoon Benedictine
Stir well with cracked Ice and strain into 3 oz. Cocktail glass.

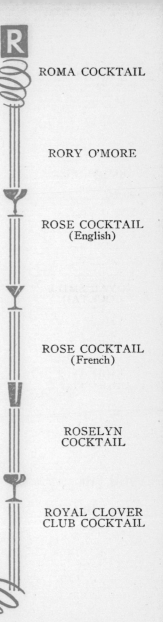

ROMA COCKTAIL

1 oz. Old Mr. Boston Dry Gin
1/2 oz. French Vermouth
1/2 oz. Italian Vermouth
Add 2 or 3 Strawberries. Shake well
with cracked Ice and strain into 3 oz.
Cocktail glass.

RORY O'MORE

3/4 oz. Italian Vermouth
1 1/2 oz. Irish Whiskey
1 Dash Orange Bitters
Stir well with cracked Ice and strain
into 3 oz. Cocktail glass.

ROSE COCKTAIL
(English)

1/2 oz. Old Mr. Boston Apricot
Flavored Brandy
1/2 oz. French Vermouth
1 oz. Old Mr. Boston Dry Gin
1/2 Teaspoon Lemon Juice
1 Teaspoon Grenadine
Shake well with cracked Ice and strain
into 3 oz. Cocktail glass. Frost edge of
glass by rubbing with Lemon and dipping in Powdered Sugar.

ROSE COCKTAIL
(French)

1/2 oz. Old Mr. Boston Wild
Cherry Flavored Brandy
1/2 oz. French Vermouth
1 1/4 oz. Old Mr. Boston Dry Gin
Stir well with cracked Ice and strain
into 3 oz. Cocktail glass.

ROSELYN COCKTAIL

3/4 oz. French Vermouth
1 1/2 oz. Old Mr. Boston Dry Gin
1/2 Teaspoon Grenadine
Stir well with cracked Ice and strain
into 3 oz. Cocktail glass. Twist of
Lemon Peel on top and drop in glass.

ROYAL CLOVER CLUB COCKTAIL

Juice 1 Lime
1 Tablespoon Grenadine
Yolk 1 Egg
1 1/2 oz. Old Mr. Boston Dry Gin
Shake well with cracked Ice and strain
into 4 oz. Cocktail glass.

123

R

ROYAL COCKTAIL

1 Whole Egg
Juice 1/2 Lemon
1 Teaspoon Powdered Sugar
1 1/2 oz. Old Mr. Boston Dry Gin
Shake well with cracked Ice and strain into 4 oz. Cocktail glass.

ROYAL FIZZ

Juice 1/2 Lemon
1 Teaspoon Powdered Sugar
2 oz. Old Mr. Boston Dry Gin
1 Whole Egg
Shake well with cracked Ice and strain into 8 oz. Highball glass. Fill with Carbonated Water.

ROYAL SMILE COCKTAIL

Juice 1/4 Lemon
1 Teaspoon Grenadine
1/2 oz. Old Mr. Boston Dry Gin
1 oz. Applejack
Stir well with cracked Ice and strain into 3 oz. Cocktail glass.

RUBY FIZZ

Juice 1/2 Lemon
1 Teaspoon Powdered Sugar
White of 1 Egg
1 Teaspoon Grenadine
2 oz. Old Mr. Boston Sloe Gin
Shake well with cracked Ice and strain into 8 oz. Highball glass. Fill with Carbonated Water.

RUM COBBLER

1 Teaspoon Powdered Sugar
2 oz. Carbonated Water
Fill 8 oz. Goblet with Shaved Ice
Add 2 oz. Old Mr. Boston Imported Rum
Stir well and decorate with fruits in season. Serve with straws.

Juice 1 Lime
1 Teaspoon Powdered Sugar
2 oz. Old Mr. Boston Imported Rum
Pour into 12 oz. Tom Collins glass.
Add several Cubes of Ice, fill with
Carbonated Water and stir well. Decorate with slice of Lemon and a
Cherry and drop Lime in glass. Serve
with straws.

RUM COLLINS

Into 12 oz. Tom Collins glass, put:
1/2 Teaspoon Powdered Sugar
  2 oz. Carbonated Water, and stir
    Fill glass with Cracked Ice and
    add:
  2 oz. Old Mr. Boston Imported Rum
    Fill with Carbonated Water or
    Ginger Ale
Insert spiral of Orange or Lemon Peel
(or both) and dangle end over rim of
glass.

RUM COOLER

Juice of 1/2 Lemon
1/2 Teaspoon Powdered Sugar
  1 Teaspoon Raspberry Syrup or
    Grenadine
  2 oz. Old Mr. Boston Imported Rum
Shake well with cracked Ice and strain
into Stein or 8 oz. Metal cup. Add
Cube of Ice and decorate with fruit.

RUM DAISY

1 Egg
1 Teaspoon Powdered Sugar
2 oz. Old Mr. Boston Imported Rum
  Fill glass with Milk
Shake well with cracked Ice and strain
into 12 oz. Tom Collins glass. Grate
Nutmeg on top.

RUM EGG NOGG

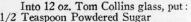

125

R

RUM FIX

Juice 1/2 Lemon or 1 Lime
1 Teaspoon Powdered Sugar
1 Teaspoon Water and stir
Fill glass with Shaved Ice
2 1/2 oz. Old Mr. Boston Imported Rum

Use 12 oz. Tom Collins glass. Stir well. Add slice of Lemon. Serve with straws.

RUM HIGHBALL

1 Cube of Ice
2 oz. Old Mr. Boston Imported Rum
Fill 8 oz. Highball glass with Ginger Ale or Carbonated Water. Add twist of Lemon Peel, if desired, and stir gently.

RUM MILK PUNCH

1 Teaspoon Powdered Sugar
2 oz. Old Mr. Boston Imported Rum
1/2 pt. Milk
Shake well with cracked Ice, strain into 12 oz. Tom Collins glass and grate Nutmeg on top.

RUM RICKEY

1 Cube of Ice
Juice 1/2 Lime
1 1/2 oz. Old Mr. Boston Imported Rum

Fill 8 oz. Highball glass with Carbonated Water and stir. Leave Lime in glass.

RUM SMASH

Muddle 1 Lump of Sugar with
1 oz. Carbonated Water and
4 Sprigs of Green Mint
Add 2 oz. Old Mr. Boston Imported Rum, then a Cube of Ice

Stir and decorate with a slice of Orange and a Cherry. Twist Lemon Peel on top. Use Old Fashioned Cocktail glass.

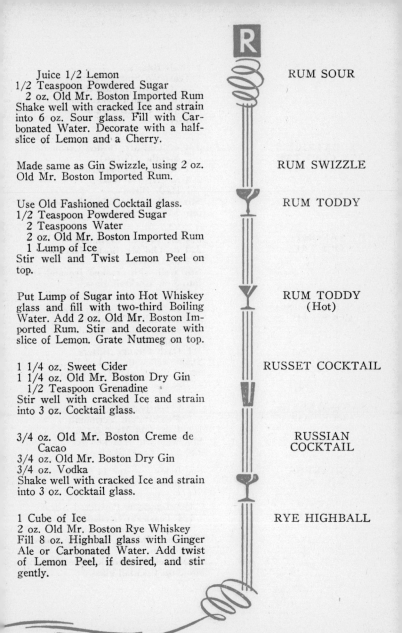

R

Juice 1/2 Lemon
1/2 Teaspoon Powdered Sugar
2 oz. Old Mr. Boston Imported Rum
Shake well with cracked Ice and strain into 6 oz. Sour glass. Fill with Carbonated Water. Decorate with a half-slice of Lemon and a Cherry.

RUM SOUR

Made same as Gin Swizzle, using 2 oz. Old Mr. Boston Imported Rum.

RUM SWIZZLE

Use Old Fashioned Cocktail glass.
1/2 Teaspoon Powdered Sugar
2 Teaspoons Water
2 oz. Old Mr. Boston Imported Rum
1 Lump of Ice
Stir well and Twist Lemon Peel on top.

RUM TODDY

Put Lump of Sugar into Hot Whiskey glass and fill with two-third Boiling Water. Add 2 oz. Old Mr. Boston Imported Rum. Stir and decorate with slice of Lemon. Grate Nutmeg on top.

RUM TODDY
(Hot)

1 1/4 oz. Sweet Cider
1 1/4 oz. Old Mr. Boston Dry Gin
1/2 Teaspoon Grenadine
Stir well with cracked Ice and strain into 3 oz. Cocktail glass.

RUSSET COCKTAIL

3/4 oz. Old Mr. Boston Creme de Cacao
3/4 oz. Old Mr. Boston Dry Gin
3/4 oz. Vodka
Shake well with cracked Ice and strain into 3 oz. Cocktail glass.

RUSSIAN COCKTAIL

1 Cube of Ice
2 oz. Old Mr. Boston Rye Whiskey
Fill 8 oz. Highball glass with Ginger Ale or Carbonated Water. Add twist of Lemon Peel, if desired, and stir gently.

RYE HIGHBALL

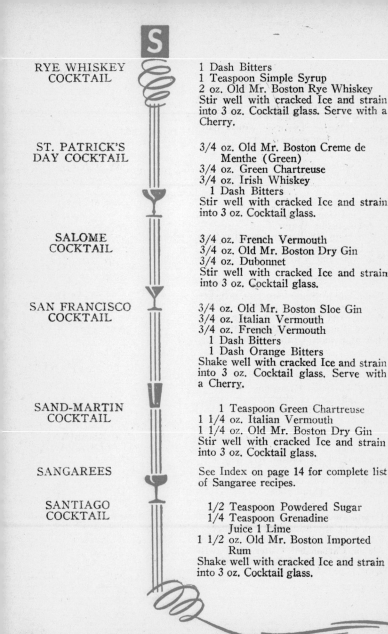

RYE WHISKEY COCKTAIL

1 Dash Bitters
1 Teaspoon Simple Syrup
2 oz. Old Mr. Boston Rye Whiskey
Stir well with cracked Ice and strain
into 3 oz. Cocktail glass. Serve with a
Cherry.

ST. PATRICK'S DAY COCKTAIL

3/4 oz. Old Mr. Boston Creme de
    Menthe (Green)
3/4 oz. Green Chartreuse
3/4 oz. Irish Whiskey
1 Dash Bitters
Stir well with cracked Ice and strain
into 3 oz. Cocktail glass.

SALOME COCKTAIL

3/4 oz. French Vermouth
3/4 oz. Old Mr. Boston Dry Gin
3/4 oz. Dubonnet
Stir well with cracked Ice and strain
into 3 oz. Cocktail glass.

SAN FRANCISCO COCKTAIL

3/4 oz. Old Mr. Boston Sloe Gin
3/4 oz. Italian Vermouth
3/4 oz. French Vermouth
1 Dash Bitters
1 Dash Orange Bitters
Shake well with cracked Ice and strain
into 3 oz. Cocktail glass. Serve with
a Cherry.

SAND-MARTIN COCKTAIL

1 Teaspoon Green Chartreuse
1 1/4 oz. Italian Vermouth
1 1/4 oz. Old Mr. Boston Dry Gin
Stir well with cracked Ice and strain
into 3 oz. Cocktail glass.

SANGAREES

See Index on page 14 for complete list
of Sangaree recipes.

SANTIAGO COCKTAIL

1/2 Teaspoon Powdered Sugar
1/4 Teaspoon Grenadine
    Juice 1 Lime
1 1/2 oz. Old Mr. Boston Imported
    Rum
Shake well with cracked Ice and strain
into 3 oz. Cocktail glass.

2 oz. Old Mr. Boston California
    Brandy
2 Dashes Bitters
1/2 Teaspoon Pineapple Syrup
1/2 Teaspoon Maraschino
Stir well with cracked Ice and strain
into 3 oz. Cocktail glass.

**SARATOGA
COCKTAIL**

Fill 12 oz. Tom Collins glass with
cracked Ice. Fill with Sarsaparilla. Insert spiral of Lemon and dangle end
over rim of glass.

**SARATOGA
COOLER**

1/2 Teaspoon Old Mr. Boston Apricot
    Flavored Brandy
1/2 Teaspoon Absinthe Substitute
2 oz. Applejack
Stir well with cracked Ice and strain
into 3 oz. Cocktail glass.

**SAUCY SUE
COCKTAIL**

Use Large Glass Pitcher
4 Teaspoons Powdered Sugar
6 oz. Carbonated Water
1/2 oz. Old Mr. Boston Triple Sec
1/2 oz. Old Mr. Boston Curacao
2 oz. Old Mr. Boston California
    Brandy
Fill pitcher with cubes of Ice. Add **1**
pint of Sauterne. Stir well and decorate with as many fruits as available
and also Rind of Cucumber inserted on
each side of pitcher. Top with small
bunch of Mint Sprigs. Serve in 5 oz.
Claret glass.

SAUTERNE CUP

Juice 1/2 Lime
1/2 Teaspoon Grenadine
1 3/4 oz. Old Mr. Boston Imported
    Rum
1 Twist Orange Peel
Shake well with cracked Ice and strain
into 3 oz. Cocktail glass.

SAXON COCKTAIL

S

SAZERAC
COCKTAIL

Put 1/4 Teaspoon Absinthe Substitute into an Old Fashioned Cocktail glass and revolve glass until it is entirely coated with the Absinthe Substitute. Then add:
1/2 Lump of Sugar
  2 Dashes Bitters
    Sufficient water to cover Sugar, and muddle well
  2 Cubes of Ice
  2 oz. Old Mr. Boston Rye or Bourbon Whiskey
Stir very well. Add Twist of Lemon Peel. (For best results, put glass on Ice for a few minutes before using.)

SCOTCH BISHOP
COCKTAIL

  1 oz. Scotch Whiskey
1/2 oz. Orange Juice
1/2 oz. French Vermouth
1/2 Teaspoon Old Mr. Boston Triple Sec
1/4 Teaspoon Powdered Sugar
    Twist of Lemon Peel
Shake well with cracked Ice and strain into 3 oz. Cocktail glass.

SCOTCH RICKEY

  1 Cube of Ice
    Juice 1/2 Lime
1 1/2 oz. Scotch Whiskey
Fill 8 oz. Highball glass with Carbonated Water and stir. Leave Lime in glass.

SCOTCH WHISKEY
HIGHBALL

  1 Cube of Ice
  2 oz. Scotch Whiskey
Fill 8 oz. Highball glass with Ginger Ale or Carbonated Water. Add twist of Lemon Peel, if desired, and stir gently.

Juice 1/4 Lemon
1 1/2 oz. Old Mr. Boston Dry Gin
1 Teaspoon Maraschino
3 Sprigs Fresh Mint
Shake well with cracked Ice and strain into 3 oz. Cocktail glass.

SENSATION COCKTAIL

White of 1 Egg
1 1/2 oz. Old Mr. Boston Imported Rum
Juice 1/2 Lime
1 Teaspoon Grenadine
Shake well with cracked Ice and strain into 4 oz. Cocktail glass.

SEPTEMBER MORN COCKTAIL

2 Teaspoons Grapefruit Juice
1/2 oz. Maraschino
1 1/4 oz. Old Mr. Boston Dry Gin
Shake well with cracked Ice and strain into 3 oz. Cocktail glass. Decorate with Sprig of Fresh Mint.

SEVENTH HEAVEN COCKTAIL

1/2 Teaspoon Powdered Sugar
1 Egg
1 oz. Port Wine
1 oz. Old Mr. Boston Imported Rum
Shake well with cracked Ice and strain into 4 oz. Cocktail glass.

SEVILLA COCKTAIL

1 1/2 oz. Irish Whiskey
1/2 oz. French Vermouth
1 Teaspoon Old Mr. Boston Creme de Menthe (Green)
Stir well with cracked Ice and strain into 3 oz. Cocktail glass. Serve with an Olive.

SHAMROCK COCKTAIL

5 oz. Beer
5 oz. Ginger Ale
Use 12 oz. Tom Collins glass and stir very gently.

SHANDY GAFF

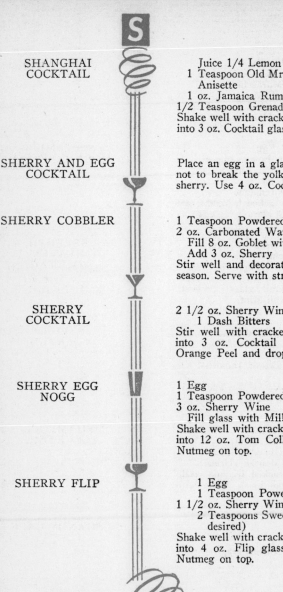

SHANGHAI COCKTAIL

Juice 1/4 Lemon
1 Teaspoon Old Mr. Boston Anisette
1 oz. Jamaica Rum
1/2 Teaspoon Grenadine
Shake well with cracked Ice and strain into 3 oz. Cocktail glass.

SHERRY AND EGG COCKTAIL

Place an egg in a glass, being careful not to break the yolk. Fill glass with sherry. Use 4 oz. Cocktail glass.

SHERRY COBBLER

1 Teaspoon Powdered Sugar
2 oz. Carbonated Water
Fill 8 oz. Goblet with Shaved Ice
Add 3 oz. Sherry
Stir well and decorate with fruits in season. Serve with straws.

SHERRY COCKTAIL

2 1/2 oz. Sherry Wine
1 Dash Bitters
Stir well with cracked Ice and strain into 3 oz. Cocktail glass. Twist of Orange Peel and drop in glass.

SHERRY EGG NOGG

1 Egg
1 Teaspoon Powdered Sugar
3 oz. Sherry Wine
Fill glass with Milk
Shake well with cracked Ice and strain into 12 oz. Tom Collins glass. Grate Nutmeg on top.

SHERRY FLIP

1 Egg
1 Teaspoon Powdered Sugar
1 1/2 oz. Sherry Wine
2 Teaspoons Sweet Cream (if desired)
Shake well with cracked Ice and strain into 4 oz. Flip glass. Grate a little Nutmeg on top.

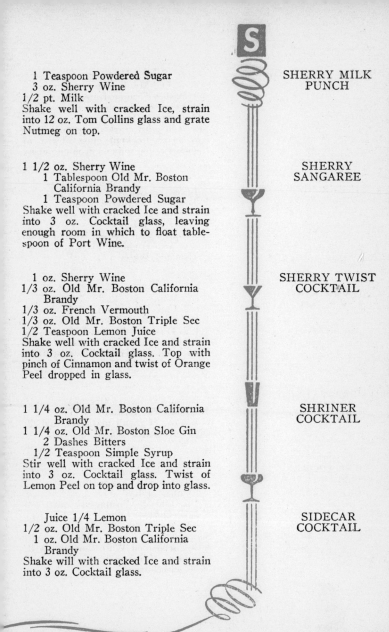

1 Teaspoon Powdered Sugar
3 oz. Sherry Wine
1/2 pt. Milk
Shake well with cracked Ice, strain into 12 oz. Tom Collins glass and grate Nutmeg on top.

SHERRY MILK PUNCH

1 1/2 oz. Sherry Wine
1 Tablespoon Old Mr. Boston California Brandy
1 Teaspoon Powdered Sugar
Shake well with cracked Ice and strain into 3 oz. Cocktail glass, leaving enough room in which to float tablespoon of Port Wine.

SHERRY SANGAREE

1 oz. Sherry Wine
1/3 oz. Old Mr. Boston California Brandy
1/3 oz. French Vermouth
1/3 oz. Old Mr. Boston Triple Sec
1/2 Teaspoon Lemon Juice
Shake well with cracked Ice and strain into 3 oz. Cocktail glass. Top with pinch of Cinnamon and twist of Orange Peel dropped in glass.

SHERRY TWIST COCKTAIL

1 1/4 oz. Old Mr. Boston California Brandy
1 1/4 oz. Old Mr. Boston Sloe Gin
2 Dashes Bitters
1/2 Teaspoon Simple Syrup
Stir well with cracked Ice and strain into 3 oz. Cocktail glass. Twist of Lemon Peel on top and drop into glass.

SHRINER COCKTAIL

Juice 1/4 Lemon
1/2 oz. Old Mr. Boston Triple Sec
1 oz. Old Mr. Boston California Brandy
Shake will with cracked Ice and strain into 3 oz. Cocktail glass.

SIDECAR COCKTAIL

SILVER COCKTAIL

1 oz. French Vermouth
1 oz. Old Mr. Boston Dry Gin
2 Dashes Orange Bitters
1/4 Teaspoon Simple Syrup
1/2 Teaspoon Maraschino
Stir well with cracked Ice and strain into 3 oz. Cocktail glass. Twist of Lemon Peel on top and drop into glass.

SILVER FIZZ

Juice 1/2 Lemon
1 Teaspoon Powdered Sugar
2 oz. Old Mr. Boston Dry Gin
White of 1 Egg
Shake well with cracked Ice and strain into 8 oz. Highball glass. Fill with Carbonated Water.

SILVER KING COCKTAIL

White of 1 Egg
Juice 1/4 Lemon
1 1/2 oz. Old Mr. Boston Dry Gin
1/2 Teaspoon Powdered Sugar
2 Dashes Orange Bitters
Shake well with cracked Ice and strain into 4 oz. Cocktail glass.

SILVER STALLION FIZZ

1 Scoop Vanilla Ice Cream
2 oz. Old Mr. Boston Dry Gin
Use 8 oz. Highball glass, stir and fill with Carbonated Water.

SINGAPORE SLING

Juice 1/2 Lemon
1 Teaspoon Powdered Sugar
2 Cubes of Ice
2 oz. Old Mr. Boston Dry Gin
1/2 oz. Old Mr. Boston Wild Cherry Flavored Brandy
Serve in 12 oz. Tom Collins glass. Fill with Carbonated Water and stir well. Decorate with fruits in season and serve with straws.

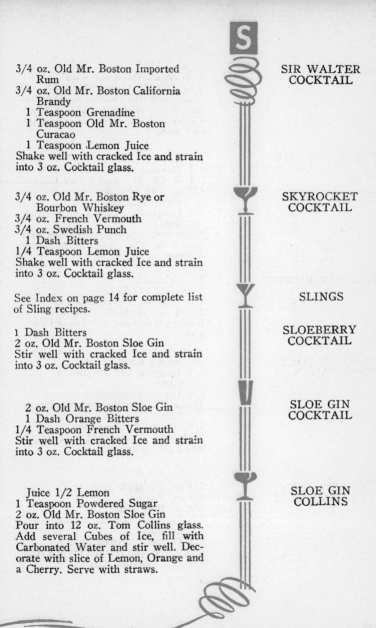

S

3/4 oz. Old Mr. Boston Imported
    Rum
3/4 oz. Old Mr. Boston California
    Brandy
  1 Teaspoon Grenadine
  1 Teaspoon Old Mr. Boston
    Curacao
  1 Teaspoon Lemon Juice
Shake well with cracked Ice and strain
into 3 oz. Cocktail glass.

SIR WALTER
COCKTAIL

3/4 oz. Old Mr. Boston Rye or
    Bourbon Whiskey
3/4 oz. French Vermouth
3/4 oz. Swedish Punch
  1 Dash Bitters
1/4 Teaspoon Lemon Juice
Shake well with cracked Ice and strain
into 3 oz. Cocktail glass.

SKYROCKET
COCKTAIL

See Index on page 14 for complete list
of Sling recipes.

SLINGS

1 Dash Bitters
2 oz. Old Mr. Boston Sloe Gin
Stir well with cracked Ice and strain
into 3 oz. Cocktail glass.

SLOEBERRY
COCKTAIL

2 oz. Old Mr. Boston Sloe Gin
  1 Dash Orange Bitters
1/4 Teaspoon French Vermouth
Stir well with cracked Ice and strain
into 3 oz. Cocktail glass.

SLOE GIN
COCKTAIL

  Juice 1/2 Lemon
1 Teaspoon Powdered Sugar
2 oz. Old Mr. Boston Sloe Gin
Pour into 12 oz. Tom Collins glass.
Add several Cubes of Ice, fill with
Carbonated Water and stir well. Decorate with slice of Lemon, Orange and
a Cherry. Serve with straws.

SLOE GIN
COLLINS

S

SLOE GIN FIZZ

Juice 1/2 Lemon
1 Teaspoon Powdered Sugar
2 oz. Old Mr. Boston Sloe Gin
Shake well with cracked Ice and strain into 8 oz. Highball glass. Fill with Carbonated Water. Decorate with slice of Lemon.

SLOE GIN FLIP

1 Egg
1 Teaspoon Powdered Sugar
1 oz. Old Mr. Boston Sloe Gin
1/2 oz. Old Mr. Boston Apricot
    Flavored Brandy
2 Teaspoons Sweet Cream (if desired)
Shake well with cracked Ice and strain into 4 oz. Flip glass. Grate a little Nutmeg on top.

SLOE GIN RICKEY

1 Cube of Ice
Juice of 1/2 Lime
2 oz. Old Mr. Boston Sloe Gin
Fill 8 oz. Highball glass with Carbonated Water and stir. Leave Lime in glass.

SLOPPY JOE'S COCKTAIL No. 1

Juice 1 Lime
1/4 Teaspoon Old Mr. Boston
    Curacao
1/4 Teaspoon Grenadine
3/4 oz. Old Mr. Boston Imported
    Rum
3/4 oz. French Vermouth
Shake well with cracked Ice and strain into 3 oz. Cocktail glass.

SLOPPY JOE'S COCKTAIL No. 2

3/4 oz. Pineapple Juice
3/4 oz. Cognac
3/4 oz. Port Wine
1/4 Teaspoon Old Mr. Boston
    Curacao
1/4 Teaspoon Grenadine
Shake well with cracked Ice and strain into 3 oz. Cocktail glass.

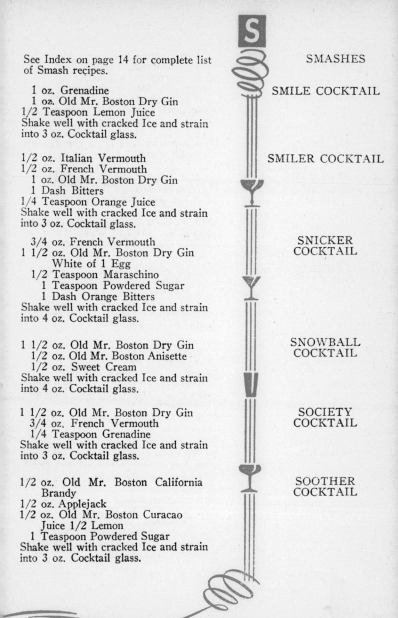

See Index on page 14 for complete list of Smash recipes.

SMASHES

SMILE COCKTAIL

1 oz. Grenadine
1 oz. Old Mr. Boston Dry Gin
1/2 Teaspoon Lemon Juice
Shake well with cracked Ice and strain into 3 oz. Cocktail glass.

SMILER COCKTAIL

1/2 oz. Italian Vermouth
1/2 oz. French Vermouth
1 oz. Old Mr. Boston Dry Gin
1 Dash Bitters
1/4 Teaspoon Orange Juice
Shake well with cracked Ice and strain into 3 oz. Cocktail glass.

SNICKER COCKTAIL

3/4 oz. French Vermouth
1 1/2 oz. Old Mr. Boston Dry Gin
White of 1 Egg
1/2 Teaspoon Maraschino
1 Teaspoon Powdered Sugar
1 Dash Orange Bitters
Shake well with cracked Ice and strain into 4 oz. Cocktail glass.

SNOWBALL COCKTAIL

1 1/2 oz. Old Mr. Boston Dry Gin
1/2 oz. Old Mr. Boston Anisette
1/2 oz. Sweet Cream
Shake well with cracked Ice and strain into 4 oz. Cocktail glass.

SOCIETY COCKTAIL

1 1/2 oz. Old Mr. Boston Dry Gin
3/4 oz. French Vermouth
1/4 Teaspoon Grenadine
Shake well with cracked Ice and strain into 3 oz. Cocktail glass.

SOOTHER COCKTAIL

1/2 oz. Old Mr. Boston California Brandy
1/2 oz. Applejack
1/2 oz. Old Mr. Boston Curacao
Juice 1/2 Lemon
1 Teaspoon Powdered Sugar
Shake well with cracked Ice and strain into 3 oz. Cocktail glass.

SOUL KISS COCKTAIL

1/4 oz. Orange Juice
1/4 oz. Dubonnet
3/4 oz. French Vermouth
3/4 oz. Old Mr. Boston Rye or
    Bourbon Whiskey
Shake well with cracked Ice and strain into 3 oz. Cocktail glass.

SOURS

See Index on page 15 for complete list of Sour recipes.

SOUTHERN GIN COCKTAIL

2 oz. Old Mr. Boston Dry Gin
2 Dashes Orange Bitters
1/2 Teaspoon Old Mr. Boston
    Curacao
Stir well with cracked Ice and strain into 3 oz. Cocktail glass. Twist of Lemon Peel on top and drop into glass.

SOUTH SIDE COCKTAIL

Juice 1/2 Lemon
1 Teaspoon Powdered Sugar
2 Sprigs Fresh Mint
1 1/2 oz. Old Mr. Boston Dry Gin
Shake well with cracked Ice and strain into 3 oz. Cocktail glass.

SOUTH SIDE FIZZ

Juice 1/2 Lemon
1 Teaspoon Powdered Sugar
2 oz. Old Mr. Boston Dry Gin
Shake well with cracked Ice and strain into 7 oz. Highball glass. Fill with Carbonated Water. Add fresh Mint Leaves.

SPANISH TOWN COCKTAIL

2 oz. Old Mr. Boston Imported Rum
1 Teaspoon Old Mr. Boston Curacao
Stir well with cracked Ice and strain into 3 oz. Cocktail glass.

SPECIAL ROUGH COCKTAIL

1 1/4 oz. Applejack
1 1/4 oz. Old Mr. Boston California
    Brandy
1/4 Teaspoon Absinthe Substitute
Stir well with cracked Ice and strain into 3 oz. Cocktail glass.

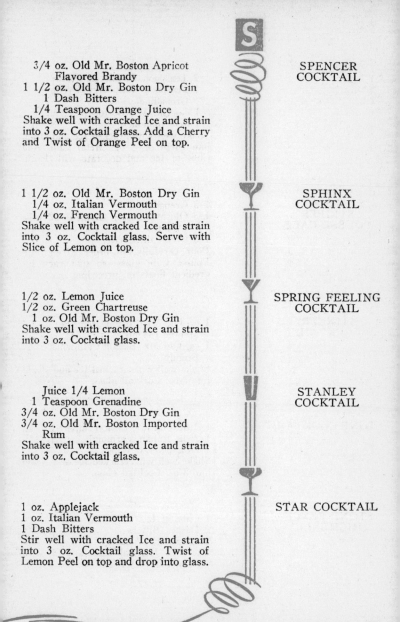

3/4 oz. Old Mr. Boston Apricot
    Flavored Brandy
1 1/2 oz. Old Mr. Boston Dry Gin
    1 Dash Bitters
1/4 Teaspoon Orange Juice
Shake well with cracked Ice and strain
into 3 oz. Cocktail glass. Add a Cherry
and Twist of Orange Peel on top.

SPENCER
COCKTAIL

1 1/2 oz. Old Mr. Boston Dry Gin
1/4 oz. Italian Vermouth
1/4 oz. French Vermouth
Shake well with cracked Ice and strain
into 3 oz. Cocktail glass. Serve with
Slice of Lemon on top.

SPHINX
COCKTAIL

1/2 oz. Lemon Juice
1/2 oz. Green Chartreuse
  1 oz. Old Mr. Boston Dry Gin
Shake well with cracked Ice and strain
into 3 oz. Cocktail glass.

SPRING FEELING
COCKTAIL

Juice 1/4 Lemon
1 Teaspoon Grenadine
3/4 oz. Old Mr. Boston Dry Gin
3/4 oz. Old Mr. Boston Imported
    Rum
Shake well with cracked Ice and strain
into 3 oz. Cocktail glass.

STANLEY
COCKTAIL

1 oz. Applejack
1 oz. Italian Vermouth
1 Dash Bitters
Stir well with cracked Ice and strain
into 3 oz. Cocktail glass. Twist of
Lemon Peel on top and drop into glass.

STAR COCKTAIL

STAR DAISY

Juice 1/2 Lemon
1/2 Teaspoon Powdered Sugar
1 Teaspoon Raspberry Syrup or Grenadine
1 oz. Old Mr. Boston Dry Gin
1 oz. Applejack
Shake well with cracked Ice and strain into Stein or 8 oz. Metal Cup. Add Cube of Ice and decorate with Fruit.

STARS AND STRIPES POUSSE CAFE

1/3 Grenadine
1/3 Old Mr. Boston Creme de Menthe (White)
1/3 Creme de Yvette
Pour carefully, in order given, into Pousse Cafe glass, so that each ingredient floats on preceding one.

STINGER COCKTAIL

1 oz. Old Mr. Boston Creme de Menthe (White)
1 oz. Old Mr. Boston California Brandy
Shake well with cracked Ice and strain into 3 oz. Cocktail glass.

STONE COCKTAIL

1/2 oz. Old Mr. Boston Imported Rum
1/2 oz. Italian Vermouth
1 oz. Sherry Wine
Shake well with cracked Ice and strain into 3 oz. Cocktail glass.

STONE FENCE HIGHBALL

1 Cube of Ice
2 Dashes Bitters
2 oz. Scotch Whiskey
Use 8 oz. Highball glass and fill with Carbonated Water, and stir gently.

3/4 oz. Old Mr. Boston Dry Gin
1 1/2 oz. Sherry Wine
Stir well with cracked Ice and strain into 3 oz. Cocktail glass.

STRAIGHT LAW COCKTAIL

1 1/2 oz. Absinthe Substitute
1/2 oz. Old Mr. Boston Anisette
White of 1 Egg
Shake well with cracked Ice and strain into 4 oz. Cocktail glass.

SUISSESSE COCKTAIL

3/4 oz. Italian Vermouth
1 1/2 oz. Old Mr. Boston Dry Gin
1 Dash Bitters
Stir well with cracked Ice and strain into 3 oz. Cocktail glass. Twist of Orange Peel on top and drop into glass.

SUNSHINE COCKTAIL

Juice 1/2 Lime
2 Cubes of Ice
2 oz. Old Mr. Boston Imported Rum
Fill 12 oz. Tom Collins glass with Ginger Ale and stir gently.

SUSIE TAYLOR

1/2 Teaspoon Absinthe Substitute
2 Dashes Bitters
3/4 oz. French Vermouth
1 1/2 oz. Old Mr. Boston Rye or Bourbon Whiskey
Shake well with cracked Ice and strain into 3 oz. Cocktail glass.

SWISS FAMILY COCKTAIL

See Index on page 15 for complete list of Swizzle recipes.

SWIZZLES

3/4 oz. Old Mr. Boston Dry Gin
3/4 oz. Italian Vermouth
3/4 oz. Green Chartreuse
1 Dash Orange Bitters
Stir well with cracked Ice and strain into 3 oz. Cocktail glass. Twist of Lemon Peel on top and serve with Cherry or Olive.

TAILSPIN COCKTAIL

141

TANGO COCKTAIL

1/2 oz. Orange Juice
1/2 oz. French Vermouth
1/2 oz. Italian Vermouth
 1 oz. Old Mr. Boston Dry Gin
1/2 Teaspoon Old Mr. Boston
   Curacao
Shake well with cracked Ice and strain
into 4 oz. Cocktail glass.

**TEMPTATION
COCKTAIL**

1 1/2 oz. Old Mr. Boston Rye or
   Bourbon Whiskey
 1/2 Teaspoon Old Mr. Boston
   Curacao
 1/2 Teaspoon Absinthe Substitute
 1/2 Teaspoon Dubonnet
  1 Twist Orange Peel
  1 Twist Lemon Peel
Shake well with cracked Ice and strain
into 3 oz. Cocktail glass.

**TEMPTER
COCKTAIL**

1 oz. Port Wine
1 oz. Old Mr. Boston Apricot
   Flavored Brandy
Shake well with cracked Ice and strain
into 3 oz. Cocktail glass.

**THANKSGIVING
SPECIAL
COCKTAIL**

3/4 oz. Old Mr. Boston Apricot
   Nectar Liqueur
3/4 oz. Old Mr. Boston Dry Gin
3/4 oz. French Vermouth
1/4 Teaspoon Lemon Juice
Shake well with cracked Ice and strain
into 3 oz. Cocktail glass. Serve with a
Cherry.

**THIRD DEGREE
COCKTAIL**

1 1/2 oz. Old Mr. Boston Dry Gin
 3/4 oz. French Vermouth
  1 Teaspoon Absinthe Substitute
Stir well with cracked Ice and strain
into 3 oz. Cocktail glass.

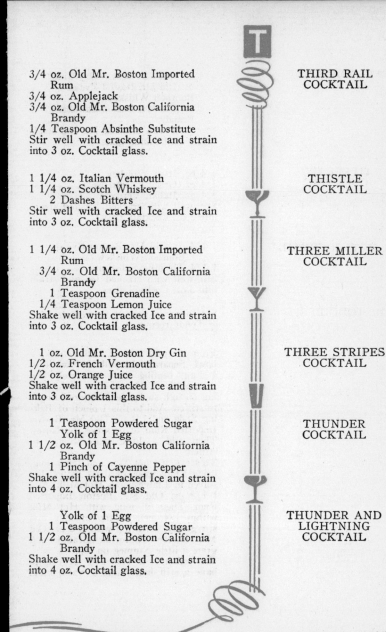

3/4 oz. Old Mr. Boston Imported
    Rum
3/4 oz. Applejack
3/4 oz. Old Mr. Boston California
    Brandy
1/4 Teaspoon Absinthe Substitute
Stir well with cracked Ice and strain
into 3 oz. Cocktail glass.

**THIRD RAIL
COCKTAIL**

1 1/4 oz. Italian Vermouth
1 1/4 oz. Scotch Whiskey
    2 Dashes Bitters
Stir well with cracked Ice and strain
into 3 oz. Cocktail glass.

**THISTLE
COCKTAIL**

1 1/4 oz. Old Mr. Boston Imported
    Rum
  3/4 oz. Old Mr. Boston California
    Brandy
  1 Teaspoon Grenadine
  1/4 Teaspoon Lemon Juice
Shake well with cracked Ice and strain
into 3 oz. Cocktail glass.

**THREE MILLER
COCKTAIL**

1 oz. Old Mr. Boston Dry Gin
1/2 oz. French Vermouth
1/2 oz. Orange Juice
Shake well with cracked Ice and strain
into 3 oz. Cocktail glass.

**THREE STRIPES
COCKTAIL**

1 Teaspoon Powdered Sugar
  Yolk of 1 Egg
1 1/2 oz. Old Mr. Boston California
    Brandy
  1 Pinch of Cayenne Pepper
Shake well with cracked Ice and strain
into 4 oz. Cocktail glass.

**THUNDER
COCKTAIL**

  Yolk of 1 Egg
  1 Teaspoon Powdered Sugar
1 1/2 oz. Old Mr. Boston California
    Brandy
Shake well with cracked Ice and strain
into 4 oz. Cocktail glass.

**THUNDER AND
LIGHTNING
COCKTAIL**

THUNDERCLAP COCKTAIL

3/4 oz. Old Mr. Boston Dry Gin
3/4 oz. Old Mr. Boston Rye or Bourbon Whiskey
3/4 oz. Old Mr. Boston California Brandy
Stir well with cracked Ice and strain into 3 oz. Cocktail glass.

TIPPERARY COCKTAIL

3/4 oz. Irish Whiskey
3/4 oz. Green Chartreuse
3/4 oz. Italian Vermouth
Stir well with cracked Ice and strain into 3 oz. Cocktail glass.

T. N. T. COCKTAIL

1 1/4 oz. Old Mr. Boston Rye or Bourbon Whiskey
1 1/4 Absinthe Substitute
Stir well with cracked Ice and strain into 3 oz. Cocktail glass.

TODDIES

See Index on page 15 for complete list of Toddy recipes.

TOM AND JERRY

First prepare batter, using mixing bowl. Separate the yolk and white of 1 Egg, beating each separately and thoroughly. Then combine both, adding enough superfine Powdered Sugar to stiffen. Add to this 1 pinch of Baking Soda and 1/4 oz. Old Mr. Boston Imported Rum to preserve the batter. Then add a little more Sugar to stiffen.

To serve, use hot Tom and Jerry mug, using 1 tablespoon of above batter, dissolved in 3 tablespoons Hot Milk. Add 1 1/2 oz. Old Mr. Boston Imported Rum. Then fill mug with Hot Milk within 1/4 inch of top of mug and stir gently. Then top with 1/2 oz. Old Mr. Boston California Brandy and grate a little Nutmeg on top.

The secret of a Tom and Jerry is to have a stiff batter and a warm mug.

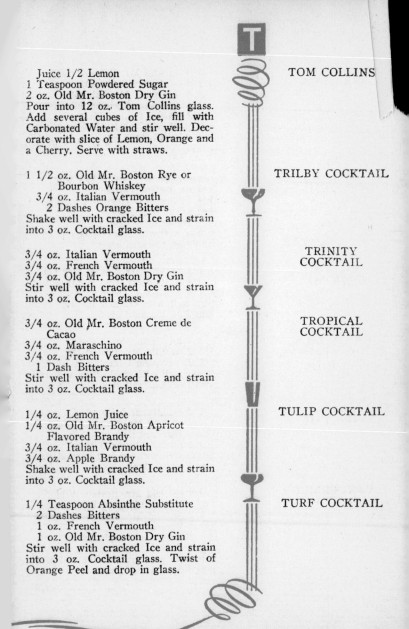

Juice 1/2 Lemon
1 Teaspoon Powdered Sugar
2 oz. Old Mr. Boston Dry Gin
Pour into 12 oz. Tom Collins glass.
Add several cubes of Ice, fill with
Carbonated Water and stir well. Decorate with slice of Lemon, Orange and
a Cherry. Serve with straws.

TOM COLLINS

1 1/2 oz. Old Mr. Boston Rye or
       Bourbon Whiskey
   3/4 oz. Italian Vermouth
    2 Dashes Orange Bitters
Shake well with cracked Ice and strain
into 3 oz. Cocktail glass.

TRILBY COCKTAIL

3/4 oz. Italian Vermouth
3/4 oz. French Vermouth
3/4 oz. Old Mr. Boston Dry Gin
Stir well with cracked Ice and strain
into 3 oz. Cocktail glass.

**TRINITY
COCKTAIL**

3/4 oz. Old Mr. Boston Creme de
       Cacao
3/4 oz. Maraschino
3/4 oz. French Vermouth
  1 Dash Bitters
Stir well with cracked Ice and strain
into 3 oz. Cocktail glass.

**TROPICAL
COCKTAIL**

1/4 oz. Lemon Juice
1/4 oz. Old Mr. Boston Apricot
       Flavored Brandy
3/4 oz. Italian Vermouth
3/4 oz. Apple Brandy
Shake well with cracked Ice and strain
into 3 oz. Cocktail glass.

TULIP COCKTAIL

1/4 Teaspoon Absinthe Substitute
  2 Dashes Bitters
  1 oz. French Vermouth
  1 oz. Old Mr. Boston Dry Gin
Stir well with cracked Ice and strain
into 3 oz. Cocktail glass. Twist of
Orange Peel and drop in glass.

TURF COCKTAIL

145

TUXEDO COCKTAIL

1 1/4 oz. Old Mr. Boston Dry Gin
1 1/4 oz. French Vermouth
1/4 Teaspoon Maraschino
1/4 Teaspoon Absinthe Substitute
2 Dashes Orange Bitters

Stir well with cracked Ice and strain into 3 oz. Cocktail glass. Serve with a Cherry.

TWIN SIX COCKTAIL

1 oz. Old Mr. Boston Dry Gin
1/2 oz. Italian Vermouth
1/4 Teaspoon Grenadine
1/2 oz. Orange Juice
White of 1 Egg

Shake well with cracked Ice and strain into 4 oz. Cocktail glass.

ULANDA COCKTAIL

1 1/2 oz. Old Mr. Boston Dry Gin
3/4 oz. Old Mr. Boston Triple Sec
1/4 Teaspoon Absinthe

Stir well with cracked Ice and strain into 3 oz. Cocktail glass.

UNION JACK COCKTAIL

3/4 oz. Creme de Yvette
1 1/2 oz. Old Mr. Boston Dry Gin
1/2 Teaspoon Grenadine

Shake well with cracked Ice and strain into 3 oz. Cocktail glass.

VALENCIA COCKTAIL

1/2 oz. Orange Juice
1 1/2 oz. Old Mr. Boston Apricot Flavored Brandy
2 Dashes Orange Bitters

Shake well with cracked Ice and strain into 3 oz. Cocktail glass.

VANDERBILT COCKTAIL

3/4 oz. Old Mr. Boston Wild Cherry Flavored Brandy
1 1/2 oz. Old Mr. Boston California Brandy
1 Teaspoon Simple Syrup
2 Dashes Bitters

Stir well with cracked Ice and strain into 3 oz. Cocktail glass.

1 1/2 oz. Old Mr. Boston Dry Gin
  3/4 oz. Rhubarb Syrup
Shake well with cracked Ice and strain into 3 oz. Cocktail glass. Serve with Sprig of Fresh Mint.

VEGETARIAN GIN COCKTAIL

  3/4 oz. Creme de Cassis
1 1/2 oz. French Vermouth
  1 Cube of Ice
Fill 8 oz. Highball glass with Carbonated Water and stir.

VERMOUTH CASSIS

1 oz. French Vermouth
1 oz. Italian Vermouth
1 Dash Orange Bitters
Stir well with cracked Ice and strain into 3 oz. Cocktail glass. Serve with a Cherry.

VERMOUTH COCKTAIL

  1/2 oz. Old Mr. Boston Dry Gin
1 1/4 oz. Italian Vermouth
  1/2 oz. Old Mr. Boston California Brandy
Stir well with cracked Ice and strain into 3 oz. Cocktail glass.

VICTOR COCKTAIL

  Juice 1/2 Lemon
  1/2 Teaspoon Powdered Sugar
1 1/2 oz. Old Mr. Boston Dry Gin
  1/2 oz. Creme de Yvette
Shake well with cracked Ice and strain into 7 oz. Highball glass. Fill with Carbonated Water.

VIOLET FIZZ

1 1/4 oz. French Vermouth
1 1/4 oz. Old Mr. Boston Dry Gin
  1 Teaspoon Old Mr. Boston Curacao
Stir well with cracked Ice and strain into 3 oz. Cocktail glass.

WALLICK COCKTAIL

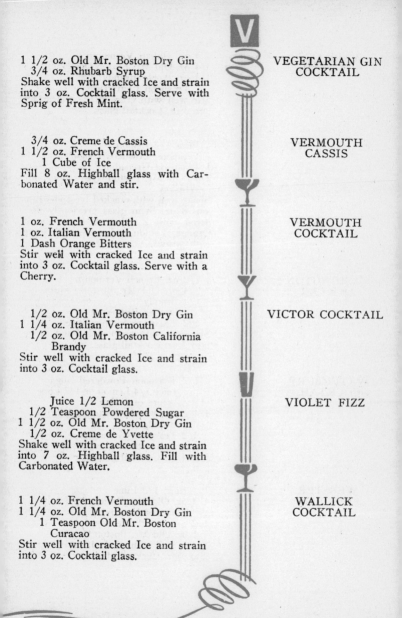

WARDAY'S COCKTAIL

3/4 oz. Italian Vermouth
3/4 oz. Old Mr. Boston Dry Gin
3/4 oz. Apple Brandy
1 Teaspoon Chartreuse
Stir well with cracked Ice and strain into 3 oz. Cocktail glass.

WARD EIGHT

Juice 1/2 Lemon
1 Teaspoon Powdered Sugar
1 Teaspoon Grenadine
2 oz. Old Mr. Boston Rye or Bourbon Whiskey
Shake well with cracked Ice and strain into 8 oz. Stem glass previously prepared with 2 cubes of Ice, slice of Orange, Lemon and a Cherry. Serve with straws.

WASHINGTON COCKTAIL

1 1/2 oz. French Vermouth
3/4 oz. Old Mr. Boston California Brandy
2 Dashes Bitters
1/2 Teaspoon Simple Syrup
Stir well with cracked Ice and strain into 3 oz. Cocktail glass.

WATERBURY COCKTAIL

1/2 Teaspoon Powdered Sugar
Juice 1/4 Lemon or 1/2 Lime
White of 1 Egg
1 1/2 oz. Old Mr. Boston California Brandy
1/2 Teaspoon Grenadine
Shake well with cracked Ice and strain into 4 oz. Cocktail glass.

WEBSTER COCKTAIL

Juice 1/2 Lime
1/4 oz. Old Mr. Boston Apricot Flavored Brandy
1/2 oz. French Vermouth
1 oz. Old Mr. Boston Dry Gin
Shake well with cracked Ice and strain into 3 oz. Cocktail glass.

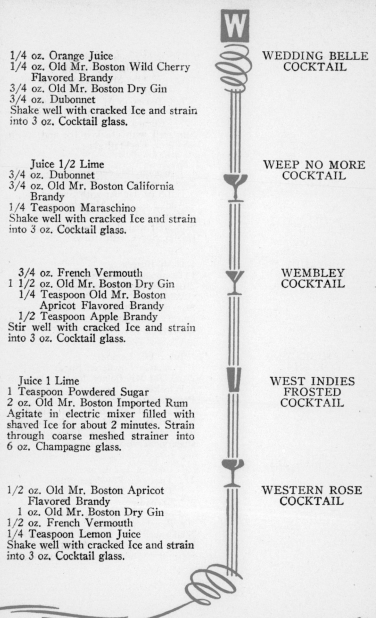

1/4 oz. Orange Juice
1/4 oz. Old Mr. Boston Wild Cherry
    Flavored Brandy
3/4 oz. Old Mr. Boston Dry Gin
3/4 oz. Dubonnet
Shake well with cracked Ice and strain
into 3 oz. Cocktail glass.

WEDDING BELLE COCKTAIL

    Juice 1/2 Lime
3/4 oz. Dubonnet
3/4 oz. Old Mr. Boston California
    Brandy
1/4 Teaspoon Maraschino
Shake well with cracked Ice and strain
into 3 oz. Cocktail glass.

WEEP NO MORE COCKTAIL

3/4 oz. French Vermouth
1 1/2 oz. Old Mr. Boston Dry Gin
    1/4 Teaspoon Old Mr. Boston
      Apricot Flavored Brandy
    1/2 Teaspoon Apple Brandy
Stir well with cracked Ice and strain
into 3 oz. Cocktail glass.

WEMBLEY COCKTAIL

    Juice 1 Lime
1 Teaspoon Powdered Sugar
2 oz. Old Mr. Boston Imported Rum
Agitate in electric mixer filled with
shaved Ice for about 2 minutes. Strain
through coarse meshed strainer into
6 oz. Champagne glass.

WEST INDIES FROSTED COCKTAIL

1/2 oz. Old Mr. Boston Apricot
    Flavored Brandy
    1 oz. Old Mr. Boston Dry Gin
1/2 oz. French Vermouth
1/4 Teaspoon Lemon Juice
Shake well with cracked Ice and strain
into 3 oz. Cocktail glass.

WESTERN ROSE COCKTAIL

WHIP COCKTAIL

1/2 oz. French Vermouth
1/2 oz. Italian Vermouth
1 1/4 oz. Old Mr. Boston California Brandy
1/4 Teaspoon Absinthe Substitute
1 Teaspoon Old Mr. Boston Curacao

Stir well with cracked Ice and strain into 3 oz. Cocktail glass.

WHISKEY COBBLER

1 Teaspoon Powdered Sugar
2 oz. Carbonated Water
Fill 8 oz. Goblet with Shaved Ice
Add 2 oz. Old Mr. Boston Rye or Bourbon Whiskey

Stir well and decorate with fruits in season. Serve with straws.

WHISKEY COCKTAIL

1 Dash Bitters
1 Teaspoon Simple Syrup
2 oz. Old Mr. Boston Rye or Bourbon Whiskey

Stir well with cracked Ice and strain into 3 oz. Cocktail glass. Serve with a Cherry.

WHISKEY COLLINS

Juice 1/2 Lemon
1 Teaspoon Powdered Sugar
2 oz. Old Mr. Boston Rye or Bourbon Whiskey

Pour into 12 oz. Tom Collins glass. Add several cubes of Ice, fill with Carbonated Water and stir well. Decorate with slice of Lemon, Orange and a Cherry. Serve with straws.

WHISKEY DAISY

Juice of 1/2 Lemon
1/2 Teaspoon Powdered Sugar
1 Teaspoon Raspberry Syrup or Grenadine
2 oz. Old Mr. Boston Rye or Bourbon Whiskey

Shake well with cracked Ice and strain into Stein or 8 oz. Metal cup. Add cube of Ice and decorate with fruit.

1 Egg
1 Teaspoon Powdered Sugar
2 oz. Old Mr. Boston Rye or Bourbon
  Whiskey
  Fill glass with Milk
Shake well with cracked Ice and strain
into 12 oz. Tom Collins glass. Grate
Nutmeg on top.

WHISKEY EGG NOGG

Juice 1/2 Lemon
1 Teaspoon Powdered Sugar
1 Teaspoon Water and stir
  Fill glass with Shaved Ice
2 1/2 oz. Old Mr. Boston Rye or
  Bourbon Whiskey
Use 12 oz. Tom Collins glass. Stir
well. Add slice of Lemon. Serve with
straws.

WHISKEY FIX

1 Egg
1 Teaspoon Powdered Sugar
1 1/2 oz. Old Mr. Boston Rye or
  Bourbon Whiskey
2 Teaspoons Sweet Cream (if
  desired)
Shake well with cracked Ice and strain
into 4 oz. Flip glass. Grate a little
Nutmeg on top.

WHISKEY FLIP

1 Cube of Ice
2 oz. Old Mr. Boston Rye or Bourbon
  Whiskey
Fill 8 oz. Highball glass with Ginger
Ale or Carbonated Water. Add twist
of Lemon Peel, if desired, and stir
gently.

WHISKEY HIGHBALL

1 Teaspoon Powdered Sugar
2 oz. Old Mr. Boston Rye or
  Bourbon Whiskey
1/2 pt. Milk
Shake well with cracked Ice, strain
into 12 oz. Tom Collins glass and grate
Nutmeg on top.

WHISKEY MILK PUNCH

WHISKEY ORANGE	Juice 1/2 Orange 1 Teaspoon Powdered Sugar 1/2 Teaspoon Absinthe Substitute 1 1/2 oz. Old Mr. Boston Rye or Bourbon Whiskey Shake well with cracked Ice and strain into 8 oz. Highball glass. Decorate with Slice of Orange and Lemon.
WHISKEY RICKEY	1 Cube of Ice Juice of 1/2 Lime 1 1/2 oz. Old Mr. Boston Rye or Bourbon Whiskey Fill 8 oz. Highball glass with Carbonated Water and stir. Leave Lime in glass.
WHISKEY SANGAREE	1 1/2 oz. Old Mr. Boston Rye or Bourbon Whiskey 1 Teaspoon Powdered Sugar Shake well with cracked Ice and strain into 3 oz. Cocktail glass, leaving enough room in which to float a tablespoon of Port Wine.
WHISKEY SKIN	Put Lump of Sugar into Hot Whiskey glass and fill with two-thirds Boiling Water. Add 2 oz. Old Mr. Boston Rye or Bourbon Whiskey. Stir, then add Twist of Lemon Peel on top and drop in glass.
WHISKEY SLING	Dissolve 1 Teaspoon Powdered Sugar in Teaspoon of Water 2 oz. Old Mr. Boston Rye or Bourbon Whiskey 2 Cubes of Ice Serve in Old Fashioned Cocktail glass and stir. Twist of Lemon Peel on top and drop in glass.

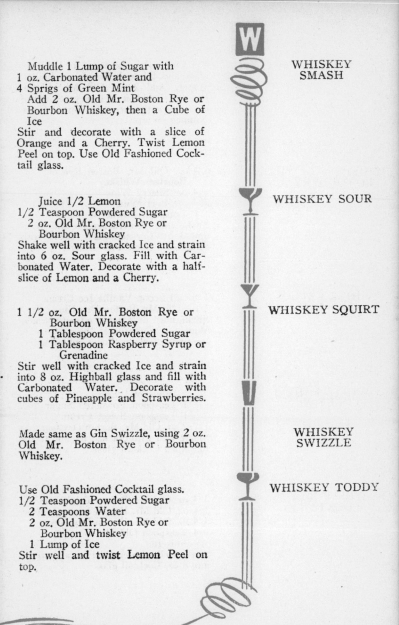

Muddle 1 Lump of Sugar with
1 oz. Carbonated Water and
4 Sprigs of Green Mint
　Add 2 oz. Old Mr. Boston Rye or
　Bourbon Whiskey, then a Cube of
　Ice
Stir and decorate with a slice of
Orange and a Cherry. Twist Lemon
Peel on top. Use Old Fashioned Cock-
tail glass.

WHISKEY SMASH

　Juice 1/2 Lemon
1/2 Teaspoon Powdered Sugar
　2 oz. Old Mr. Boston Rye or
　　Bourbon Whiskey
Shake well with cracked Ice and strain
into 6 oz. Sour glass. Fill with Carbonated Water. Decorate with a half-
slice of Lemon and a Cherry.

WHISKEY SOUR

1 1/2 oz. Old Mr. Boston Rye or
　　Bourbon Whiskey
　1 Tablespoon Powdered Sugar
　1 Tablespoon Raspberry Syrup or
　　Grenadine
Stir well with cracked Ice and strain
into 8 oz. Highball glass and fill with
Carbonated Water. Decorate with
cubes of Pineapple and Strawberries.

WHISKEY SQUIRT

Made same as Gin Swizzle, using 2 oz.
Old Mr. Boston Rye or Bourbon
Whiskey.

WHISKEY SWIZZLE

Use Old Fashioned Cocktail glass.
1/2 Teaspoon Powdered Sugar
　2 Teaspoons Water
　2 oz. Old Mr. Boston Rye or
　　Bourbon Whiskey
　1 Lump of Ice
Stir well and twist Lemon Peel on
top.

WHISKEY TODDY

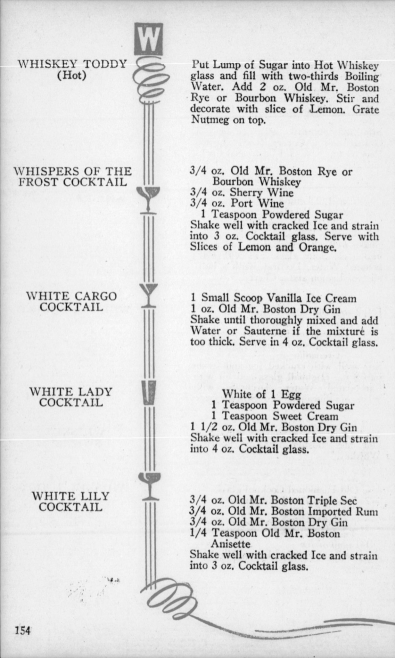

WHISKEY TODDY
(Hot)

Put Lump of Sugar into Hot Whiskey glass and fill with two-thirds Boiling Water. Add 2 oz. Old Mr. Boston Rye or Bourbon Whiskey. Stir and decorate with slice of Lemon. Grate Nutmeg on top.

WHISPERS OF THE FROST COCKTAIL

3/4 oz. Old Mr. Boston Rye or
    Bourbon Whiskey
3/4 oz. Sherry Wine
3/4 oz. Port Wine
1 Teaspoon Powdered Sugar
Shake well with cracked Ice and strain into 3 oz. Cocktail glass. Serve with Slices of Lemon and Orange.

WHITE CARGO COCKTAIL

1 Small Scoop Vanilla Ice Cream
1 oz. Old Mr. Boston Dry Gin
Shake until thoroughly mixed and add Water or Sauterne if the mixture is too thick. Serve in 4 oz. Cocktail glass.

WHITE LADY COCKTAIL

White of 1 Egg
1 Teaspoon Powdered Sugar
1 Teaspoon Sweet Cream
1 1/2 oz. Old Mr. Boston Dry Gin
Shake well with cracked Ice and strain into 4 oz. Cocktail glass.

WHITE LILY COCKTAIL

3/4 oz. Old Mr. Boston Triple Sec
3/4 oz. Old Mr. Boston Imported Rum
3/4 oz. Old Mr. Boston Dry Gin
1/4 Teaspoon Old Mr. Boston
    Anisette
Shake well with cracked Ice and strain into 3 oz. Cocktail glass.

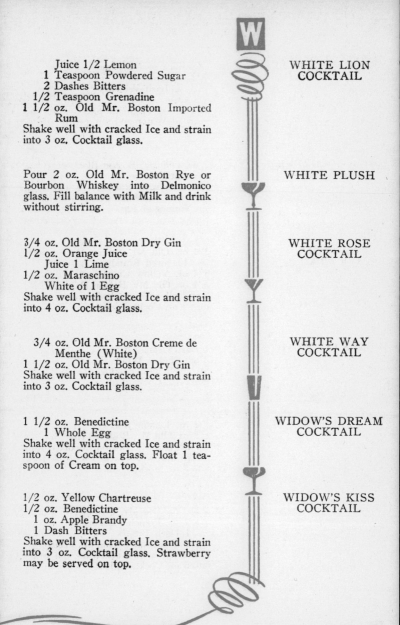

Juice 1/2 Lemon
1 Teaspoon Powdered Sugar
2 Dashes Bitters
1/2 Teaspoon Grenadine
1 1/2 oz. Old Mr. Boston Imported
Rum
Shake well with cracked Ice and strain
into 3 oz. Cocktail glass.

WHITE LION COCKTAIL

Pour 2 oz. Old Mr. Boston Rye or
Bourbon Whiskey into Delmonico
glass. Fill balance with Milk and drink
without stirring.

WHITE PLUSH

3/4 oz. Old Mr. Boston Dry Gin
1/2 oz. Orange Juice
Juice 1 Lime
1/2 oz. Maraschino
White of 1 Egg
Shake well with cracked Ice and strain
into 4 oz. Cocktail glass.

WHITE ROSE COCKTAIL

3/4 oz. Old Mr. Boston Creme de
Menthe (White)
1 1/2 oz. Old Mr. Boston Dry Gin
Shake well with cracked Ice and strain
into 3 oz. Cocktail glass.

WHITE WAY COCKTAIL

1 1/2 oz. Benedictine
1 Whole Egg
Shake well with cracked Ice and strain
into 4 oz. Cocktail glass. Float 1 teaspoon of Cream on top.

WIDOW'S DREAM COCKTAIL

1/2 oz. Yellow Chartreuse
1/2 oz. Benedictine
1 oz. Apple Brandy
1 Dash Bitters
Shake well with cracked Ice and strain
into 3 oz. Cocktail glass. Strawberry
may be served on top.

WIDOW'S KISS COCKTAIL

WILD EYED ROSE HIGHBALL

Juice of 1/2 Lime
1/2 oz. Grenadine
2 oz. Irish Whiskey
1 Cube of Ice
Fill 8 oz. Highball glass with Carbonated Water and stir gently.

WINDY CORNER COCKTAIL

2 oz. Old Mr. Boston Blackberry Flavored Brandy
Stir well with cracked Ice and strain into 3 oz. Cocktail glass. Grate a little Nutmeg on top.

XANTHIA COCKTAIL

3/4 oz. Old Mr. Boston Wild Cherry Flavored Brandy
3/4 oz. Yellow Chartreuse
3/4 oz. Old Mr. Boston Dry Gin
Stir well with cracked Ice and strain into 3 oz. Cocktail glass.

XERES COCKTAIL

1 Dash Orange Bitters
2 oz. Sherry Wine
Stir well with cracked Ice and strain into 3 oz. Cocktail glass.

X. Y. Z. COCKTAIL

1/2 oz. Lemon Juice
1/2 oz. Old Mr. Boston Triple Sec
1 oz. Old Mr. Boston Imported Rum
Shake well with cracked Ice and strain into 3 oz. Cocktail glass.

YALE COCKTAIL

1 1/2 oz. Old Mr. Boston Dry Gin
1/2 oz. French Vermouth
1 Dash Bitters
1 Teaspoon Creme de Yvette
Shake well with cracked Ice and strain into 3 oz. Cocktail glass.

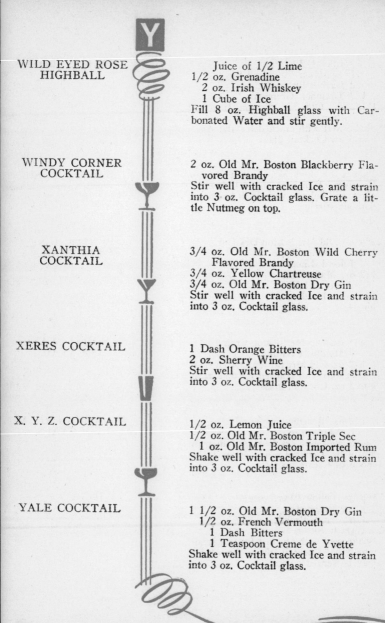

3/4 oz. Old Mr. Boston Anisette
3/4 oz. Yellow Chartreuse
3/4 oz. Old Mr. Boston Apricot
    Flavored Brandy
Stir well with cracked Ice and strain
into 3 oz. Cocktail glass.

YELLOW PARROT COCKTAIL

3/4 oz. Lemon Juice
3/4 oz. Old Mr. Boston Dry Gin
3/4 oz. French Vermouth
1/4 Teaspoon Powdered Sugar
  1 Dash Orange Bitters
Shake well with cracked Ice and strain
into 3 oz. Cocktail glass. Serve with
slice of Lemon.

ZANZIBAR COCKTAIL

1 1/2 oz. Old Mr. Boston Dry Gin
  3/4 oz. Dubonnet
    1 Twist Orange Peel
Stir well with cracked Ice and strain
into 3 oz. Cocktail glass.

ZAZA COCKTAIL

  1 oz. Passion Fruit Juice
  1 oz. Plum or Apricot Juice
    Juice 1 small Lime—drop in skin
  1 Teaspoon Powdered Sugar
  1 Dash Bitters
    Juice 1 medium-small Orange
1/2 oz. Old Mr. Boston Anisette
2 1/2 oz. Old Mr. Boston Imported
    Rum
1/2 oz. Old Mr. Boston Apricot
    Flavored Brandy
2/3 oz. Demerara Rum, 151 proof
  1 oz. Jamaica Rum
  1 oz. Porto Rican Gold Label Rum
Add cracked Ice and agitate for full
minute in Electric Mixing Machine (If
none available, shake very well in Cocktail Shaker), and strain into 14 oz.
Frosted Zombie glass. Decorate with
1/4″ square of Pineapple and 1 Green
and 1 Red Cherry, also sprig of Fresh
Mint dipped in Powdered Sugar. Serve
with straws.

ZOMBIE

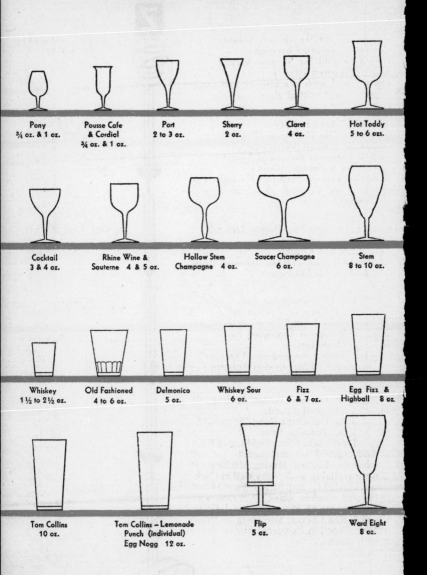

Pony
¾ oz. & 1 oz.

Pousse Cafe
& Cordial
¾ oz. & 1 oz.

Port
2 to 3 oz.

Sherry
2 oz.

Claret
4 oz.

Hot Toddy
5 to 6 ozs.

Cocktail
3 & 4 oz.

Rhine Wine &
Sauterne   4 & 5 oz.

Hollow Stem
Champagne   4 oz.

Saucer Champagne
6 oz.

Stem
8 to 10 oz.

Whiskey
1½ to 2½ oz.

Old Fashioned
4 to 6 oz.

Delmonico
5 oz.

Whiskey Sour
6 oz.

Fizz
6 & 7 oz.

Egg Fizz &
Highball   8 oz.

Tom Collins
10 oz.

Tom Collins – Lemonade
Punch (individual)
Egg Nogg   12 oz.

Flip
5 oz.

Ward Eight
8 oz.

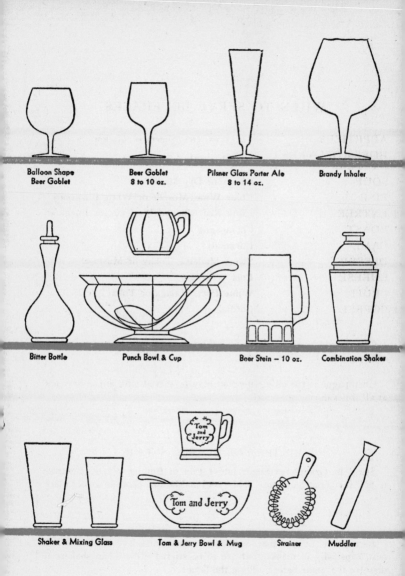

Balloon Shape
Beer Goblet

Beer Goblet
8 to 10 oz.

Pilsner Glass Porter Ale
8 to 14 oz.

Brandy Inhaler

Bitter Bottle

Punch Bowl & Cup

Beer Stein — 10 oz.

Combination Shaker

Shaker & Mixing Glass

Tom & Jerry Bowl & Mug

Strainer

Muddler

WHEN TO SERVE BEVERAGES

APPETIZER — Cocktails, Dry Sherry or Madeira

HORS-d'OEUVRES }
OYSTERS } — Moselle or White Burgundy

SOUP — Sherry or Dry Madeira

FISH — Rhine Wine, Moselle or White Burgundy

ENTREE — Light Red wines of Bordeaux or Burgundy

ROAST — Champagne

GAME — Burgundy

DESSERT — Sweet Madeira, Tokay or Muscatel

CHEESE — Port

FRUIT — White Port, Malaga or Tokay

COFFEE — Cordial

Care should be taken never to follow a sweet wine by a dry wine or a heavy wine by a light wine.

Champagne is the only wine that may be served with any course and at all times during the meal.

RECIPE FOR SIMPLE SYRUP

Stir 1 lb. Granulated Sugar into 1 Pint of Boiling Water. Continue to boil for about 5 minutes. Then cool and bottle. Store in a cool place.

Because of the fact that sugar is not easily dissolved in alcohol it is best, especially in drinks that are to be stirred rather than shaken, to dissolve the sugar before adding the liquor.